Members of Each Other

Building Community in Company With People With Developmental Disabilities

John O'Brien & Connie Lyle O'Brien

Inclusion Press

Canadian Cataloguing in Publication Data

O'Brien, John, 1946

Members of each other : building community in company with people with develpmental disabilites.

Includes bibliographical references.
ISBN 1-895418-24-0

1. Developmentally disabled. I. O'Brien, Connie Lyle.
I. Title.

HV1570.027 305.9'0816 C96-931773-5

Published by ***Inclusion Press***
24 Thome Crescent
Toronto, Ontario M6H 2S5
Canada

Preparation of this book was partially supported through a subcontract to Responsive Systems Associates from the Center on Human Policy, Syracuse University for the Research and Training Center on Community Living. The Research and Training Center on Community Living is supported through a cooperative agreement (number H133B30072) between the National Institute on Disability & Rehabilitation Research (NIDRR) and the University of Minnesota Institute on Community Integration. Members of the Center are encouraged to express their opinions; these do not necessarily represent the official position of NIDRR.

Contents

Acknowledgements

This collection is one expression of continuing conversations with friends, allies, and co-workers including Kathy Bartholomew-Lorimer, Myrna and Ed Bartlett, Barbara Buswell, Lou Chapman, Betty Ferris, Barbara Fischer, Marsha Forest, Charlie Galloway, Graham Harper, Gail Jacob, Susannah Joyce, Tom Kohler, Sandy Landis, Zana Lutfiyya, John McKnight, Beth Mount, Frieda Neumann, Viola Nimmons, Jack Pealer, Jack Pearpoint, Patricia Powell, Pat Puckett, Beth Schaffner, David Schwartz, Judith Snow, Jeff and Cindy Strully, Rebecca Shuman, Rannveig Traustadottir, Alan and Jan Tyne, John Winnenberg, and Helen Zipperlen.

Steve Taylor has provided both a steady source of insights, comments, and encouragement and, through the Center on Human Policy, the material support that makes our writing possible.

We are grateful to each of these people for the many different ways they have helped us to understand the boundaries that separate or include people with developmental disabilities.

Foreword

Te Ripowai Higgins

Hütia te rito o te harakeke	*Pluck out the centre shoot of the flax bush*
kei hea te kömako e kö?	*where would the bellbird sing?*
Rere ki uta?	*Should it fly inland?*
Rere ki tai?	*Should it fly to sea?*
Kï mai koe ki ahau	*Ask me*
He aha te mea nui o te ao?	*What is most important in the world?*
Mäku e kï atu;	*I would say;*
He tangata, he tangata,	*'Tis people, 'tis people,*
he tangata!	*'tis people*

This proverb I share from my culture, from my land, from my ancestors, the Maori (aboriginals) of Aotearoa/New Zealand. The message is simple yet powerful. It saved a village from annihilation. A member of that village, married to the chief of a powerful neighbouring tribe, used the power of words for her people and thus saved them. Proverbs by their very nature use metaphors to convey the heart of their message. They are intended to generate analysis, interpretation, reflection and ultimately action. In this case, the fact the chief chose to listen to his wife was the greatest action taken.

Flax is a familiar plant on the Aotearoa/New Zealand landscape, growing in clumps of sword-like blades in a fan formation. It has inspired many Maori proverbs, and is used as a metaphor to convey the family. The rito (centre shoot) is the child, protected on either side by it's 'parents', and the outer blades are the 'extended family'. All have a role to ensure the survival of the plant. In Maori culture grandparents/parents are not just biological, but all those generations who are collectively responsible for the nurturing and caring of the child. The grandparent's generation have special and critical responsibility for the child's mental, spiritual, educational well-being; the parents are focused on ensuring physical well-being. A typical traditional Maori whanau (extended family) can range from thirty to two hundred and thirty members. All belong and are *members of each other.*

Flax was and continues to be used by Maori for weaving and medicine, therefore care must be taken to ensure the centre three blades are protected. Lets explore this metaphor. The rito (centre shoot) is the most vulnerable member of the community. The embracing outer blades are all critical for it's well-being. When blades are cut for weaving, only the very outer blades are removed. Like the extended family, flax has many blades, each with it's own distinctive character and place in embracing the most vulnerable of their community. As with life, so comes death; the soil gets nourishment and the root system remains healthy. Those departed continue to play an important part in the life of the vulnerable. They are the guides, the exemplars.

The bellbird (an outsider) is also an integral part of this community. When it seeks nourishment from the flower, it pollinates and strengthens the plant with new genes, new gifts. Like the bellbird, the citizen advocate or friend *"..is unpaid and independent of human services, creates a relationship with a person who is vulnerable . . . bringing forward their partner's gifts..."*

The power to decide the fate of this plant belongs to the human element - the weavers. Our weavers are like sympathetic system administrators. They have power - and in setting guidelines, they shape whether the flax (or people) will be "clear cut", or given the chance to learn with future generations. The weavers, with their customs and cultural practices, set the framework, remind us of opportunities, and hopefully ensure that the flax survives.

A weaver can turn flax into an ordinary object - or fine piece of art. A system administrator can manage the warehouse - or create opportunities for human magic and art. We can create circles where **All** benefit and learn, and the place of each is respected. We can be **Members of Each Other.**

Nevertheless, I must pose the unthinkable question. What if another better, stronger, more durable material is discovered? Will the weaver relinquish their relationship in this cycle? Will we abandon the flax and drain the swamp? Will we abandon the weaver? Before we leap, the proverb teaches us to stop and think. That is the purpose of the proverb - to continually challenge and remind us of the consequences of our actions.

I couldn't help but reflect on this proverb when I read **Members of Each Other** *Building Community in Company With People With Developmental Disabilities.* John O'Brien and Connie Lye O'Brien have chosen to focus on people with developmental disabilities, nevertheless it has the same powerful message for ALL who are vulnerable. It is a universal message, one that transverses the oceans. I wonder if there is in some small corner of this world just one community that has escaped the contamination of individualization.

Today Maori are struggling to maintain their traditional society and natural community - the whanau (extended family). One hundred and sixty years of colonization and assimilation policies have driven our culture to the brink of destruction. It hangs by a thread. The more communities have become isolated from each other, the more the spirit of defiance and resistance is becoming the renaissance of Maori culture. We understand this by learning from another proverb;

He tihi maunga e pikihia	*Mountain summits are conquered*
He tihi moana e ekehia	*Mountainous oceans are conquered*
He tihi tangata e kore	*The summits of the human spirit will*
e pikihia, e ekehia	*never be conquered*
he tapu, he tapu	*for it is sacred (unconquerable)*

It is that unconquerable spirit of the human species that needs to be strengthened. **Members of Each Other,**.. exposes the dangers of power, of isolation, of helplessness. It also challenges and gives hope for communities to take back control from the 'professionals', to themselves. This book gives tried and true tools to help build the future. As with any important project, there will be much sweat and many tears. Earlier I inferred that I did not see the people with developmental disabilities, I just saw people. That is the underlying message of **Members of Each Other**.

What is most important in this world,
'tis people, 'tis people, 'tis people'

Te Ripowai Higgins is a Senior Lecturer in Maori Studies at Te Kawa a Maui, the School of Maori Studies, Victoria University of Wellington, Aotearoa/New Zealand and is an associate of Inclusion Press.

Introduction

Growing interest in inclusion reflects growing awareness of exclusion as a problem rather than a natural state of affairs. This awareness usually begins with a sense that something important is unnecessarily lost when people with developmental disabilities grow up excluded from the web of memberships and connections that define community life, their social universe limited to the orbit of their family and the sphere of specialized services. This loss was invisible to the asylum keepers who chose to label people idiots, borrowing on ιδιωτεηξ, the word ancient Greek political thinkers used to identify a private person, one incapable of participation in the common life, such as a woman or a slave or a mental incompetent. The loss was invisible because it seemed inevitable, as it still does to many people whose daily practice separates people with developmental disabilities into special places and routines and whose account of developmental disability interprets a desire for wider social participation as a failure to accept the reality of disability.

This collection of essays and reflections on practice explores work at the boundaries between people with developmental disabilities and other community members who, except for this work, would not meet and become a part of one another's lives. This boundary work offers a perspective on disability, community, and service practice and policy which we have found it interesting to consider.

Concern to include people with developmental disabilities increases at the same time as a rising concern about the state of civic life (see, for example, Putnam, 1995). We don't think that this is coincidental. People with developmental disabilities, through their gifts as individuals and as outsiders, have a fundamental contribution to make to the regeneration of community in company with their friends and allies.

Long before it was a legal form for doing business, a company was a group of people who shared their daily bread (*pan*). The root meaning embodied in the word company (*pa*) is shared nourishment and mutual protection (Partridge, 1983). The members of support circles, the core groups animating citizen advocacy programs, and the projects aimed at opening community associations to the contributions of people with developmental disabilities are company builders in the deepest sense.

This collection presents some of what we have learned from people involved in conscious efforts to create social forms that will bridge the distance created by the stereotyped beliefs and prejudiced treatment which often hide beneath masks of benevolence or professionalism. In particular, we describe initiatives aimed at...

...linking people one-to-one (citizen advocacy)

...gathering people around helping a person define and pursue a desirable future (circle of support)

... assisting people to pursue their interests as members of community associations (connecting people to community associations)

There is also a reflection on some of the ways these efforts fit with other conscious efforts to build community, efforts which are not focused on the relationship between disabled and non-disabled people.

We have included three kinds of writing in this collection. There are three essays, one on social support (or natural support as it is sometimes known), another on friendship, and the third on the personal commitments and involvements that seem to make up a good life. There are four reflections which set the boundary work we are interested in different contexts. Two of these reflections are based on program evaluations. One describes the role of circles of support in making a change from group living to individual supported living and the other reviews what another agency has learned from a concerted investment in connecting people to community associations. The third and fourth reflections arise from retreats with people who are working to facilitate circles of support and people who are involved in a variety of efforts to strengthen community in a particular place. Finally, there is a set of principles for action that have guided the development of citizen advocacy programs.

The chapters in this collection were written at different times and, apart from minor editing, we have left them as we wrote them.

Each provides a different window on the work of shifting the boundaries of exclusion.

Our method is simple: we locate people with developmental disabilities who have been involved in an important change, ask involved people to tell us their stories of how the change happened, invite their reflections on what was most important in making the change, look for common images and themes across stories of change, re-read the stories through different theoretical lenses, and, finally, re-tell the story and ask the original story tellers to correct or extend our account of the changes they have made. Clearly this method does not produce singular techniques or manuals of procedure for community building. Instead, it offers multiple ways to conceive action.

Of course, ours is far from the whole story. Our colleagues at The Center on Human Policy have collected their studies of community life from the point of view of the involved people with disabilities, families, and community members in *The Variety of Community Experience: Qualitative Studies of Family and Community Life* (Taylor, Bogdan, & Lutfiyya, 1995), a book that provides an essential complement to this one. Our friends at the Centre for Integrated Education and Community have vividly described what life at this boundary is like from the inside in *From Behind the Piano* (Pearpoint, 1990) and *What's Really Worth Doing and How To Do It* (Snow, 1994).

Members of Each Other

The way we are, we are members of each other. All of us. Everything. The difference ain't in who is a member and who is not, but in who knows it and who don't.

*-Burley Coulter**

What can it mean to know that we are members of each other? In his stories of the Port William membership, Wendell Berry hangs the possibility of civic life on the answer people make to this question.

People experience different ways of belonging to each other. They speak of others as kin, as friends, as co-workers, as neighbors, as belonging to the same association or congregation, as sharing a common interest, as being "regulars" (like a regular customer in a tavern or a regular visitor to a park). Shaped by culture and personal history, each of these different relationships implies privileges and obligations specific to its participants. Most everyone identifies someone as a friend, but each friendship takes its own shape and meaning. For each person, these different kinds of belonging form the context for social support.

Good lives for people with severe disabilities depend on whether they are recognized as members of the social networks and associations that constitute community. People recognized as members benefit from everyday exchanges of support that create opportunities to play socially valued roles and chances to form personally significant relationships. People excluded from membership risk loneliness, isolation, and powerlessness.

Because people with severe disabilities cannot take membership for granted, those concerned to build stronger, more inclusive communities must consider how some people deny other people

* A character in Wendell Berry's (1986) *The Wild Birds* (p. 136)

membership, the resources that membership can offer, and the ways membership can be established.

Mostly, knowledge of our membership in each other lies beneath words, in everyday habits. People spontaneously acknowledge membership in culture, neighborhood, association, and family through signs and rituals that signal belonging and set common boundaries. People say "we" with nuances of behavior from their way of telling visitors good-bye to their way of offering a friend help.

...let all of us speak the truth to our neighbors, for we are members of one another. Be angry, but do not sin; do not let the sun go down on your anger, and do not make room for the devil. Thieves must give up stealing; rather let them labor and work honestly with their own hands, so as to have something to share with the needy. Let no evil talk come out of your mouths, but only that which is useful for building up,... Put away from you all bitterness and wrath and anger and wrangling and slander, together with all malice, and be kind to one another, tenderhearted, forgiving one another as God has forgiven you.

-Ephesians 4: 25-32

People usually stop to speak about membership only when it becomes problematic in some way. They look for words when they believe their conduct disturbs a common sense of obligation (as Burley Coulter does in *The Wild Birds*), or when they look for a way that people disconnected from one another can form a larger membership (as Paul does when he writes to the Ephesians in the letter Burley Coulter echoes). If people try to talk about shared membership, it's hard to find words that adequately match feelings of belonging or exclusion.

Probably this poverty of language reflects cultural devaluation of relationships (Gilligan, 1982). Maybe, it shows that our language has evolved more slowly than our collective need to think explicitly about the kind of relationships that past generations of humans might have taken for granted. Anyway, the search for adequate terms becomes more difficult the more one's pattern of memberships diverges from Burley Coulter's. In Wendell Berry's stories, his memberships grow from his lifework of farming in and around a small village. He knows the history of most of the people he belongs with. He meets the same people in different contexts of membership, exchanging farm work with men alongside whom he hunts and socializes. Unlike Burley Coulter, many people rely significantly on cars and telephones to maintain their social worlds. Their different memberships occur in widely separated locations. They know little of other's history beyond the particular circumstances of their meeting. Their social networks include many people who would be strangers to one another if they happened to meet. Such loosely tied and dispersed memberships form the context for important personal relationships and mutual obligations the same as more tightly linked networks do. But they are hard to talk about.

The difficulty of finding words to reflect the web of connections that sustain our lives can be awkward in personal conversation. But when talking face to face people can repair imperfect communication with redundancy, metaphor, inflection, and movement. When words fail, we get by with inarticulate gestures or poems.

However, the lack of words to speak about and thus understand shared membership becomes crippling when people enact policies whose effects depend fundamentally on the nature of social relationships. Here, unwillingness to constructively face our inarticulateness hurts. Of US policies designed to alleviate poverty, strengthen families, deinstitutionalize, assist elders, and prevent mental and physical maladies, Seymour Sarason and his associates (1977) observe:

> *...the failure, absolute or relative, of most programs in human service (and the resulting cynicism about mounting any successful program) is in large measure due to unexamined, oversimple, and invalid conceptions of the nature, extent, and bases of human relationships. (14)*

Of British policies designed to increase community care for elders and disabled people, Martin Bulmer (1987) says:

> *...in significant respects, 'community care' policies rest upon fallacious common sense assumptions which are wrongly presented by policy makers as sociological truths. As a result there is a vacuum at the heart of care policy which is likely to lead to ineffective or deteriorating provision of services... (ix)*

The moral seems simple. To reduce the chance of unpleasant and dispiriting policy outcomes, learn more of the nature, extent, and bases of social relationships. Sensible as it may be, this injunction is less academic than it is epic: not "Go to the library, do the needed research, and bring me back the unshakable facts." but, "Bring me the ruby slippers." Earning significant knowledge of important social relationships means learning a bit at a time, through reflection on action which tests character at least as much as intellect.

Like others excluded and oppressed by shared denial of membership in each other, people with severe disabilities can teach a good deal about the social relationships at the foundation of civic life. To learn, one need only get involved: listen, look, try to understand situations in terms of shared humanity, and respond actively to invitations for personal engagement and civic action. Through this discipline, people with disabilities teach on three topics:

- The consequences of long term exclusion from membership
- The benefits implicit in recognition as a member
- Some of the explicit work necessary to change patterns of exclusion so that a person moves to being known and treated as a member

Membership denied: The consequences of exclusion

Michael* lived in an Ontario provincial institution before moving into a community residence, a job in a market, and an active role in a self advocacy group.

He remembers life in the institution as organized around control. "The *worst thing ...was havin' staff around all the time. Not goin' anywhere without staff. Doin' things they wanted you to do, not what you wanted. And gettin' blamed for stuff."* (p. 40)

And punishments: *"They made you dig for worms. It's a punishment... You hadda put your face right in the ground and dig worms, then you hadda put 'em back when you was through..." (p. 41) "I'm thanking God they're closin' that place... How would you like somebody to strip you bare naked and make you walk round the floor, around and around? I don't know why they did that, they were crazy..."* (p. 38)

Though his life has changed remarkably for the better, his experiences have left their mark: *"The scare is still in me after all these years."* (p. 38) (Melberg-Schwier, 1990)

Seymour, a professor of psychology, began his career at Southbury Training School, an innovative institution in his day. Reflecting on residents' desire to return home despite the "obviously" superior living conditions at the institution, he notes that, at the time, he considered this desire a symptom of retardation, *"...paternalism rendered you incapable of grasping and comprehending the world as it is experienced by those for whom you feel responsible... You thought you were explaining human behavior, unaware that the explanation rested on an unexamined axiom: we and they had nothing in common. If we were in their place, we would get on our knees and thank God that we were placed at Southbury. Yes, the residents were human, but we could not accord them feelings and longings that follow separation...* "(p. 149) (Sarason, 1988)

Both Michael's terror of mindless, dehumanizing control and Seymour's missed opportunity for understanding arise from their unthinking participation in settings that enact the moral exclusion of people. Such places discourage those employed as staff from knowing that they and their charges are members of one another. At the same time, these places reinforce the physical and social distance between their inmates and those people others easily recognize as "one of us." By so doing, they enforce and ratify the perception that people with severe disabilities should live outside the boundary of membership. Inside the boundary, people may dislike or disapprove of one another, people may have conflicts, people may avoid one another, and people may let one another down. But within the boundary of acknowledged membership, people see one another as approximately equal, they see the possibility of mutuality, and they consider others entitled to fair treatment and a share in common resources.

The conflict between some parents of severely disabled children and some of their professional advisers highlights the contrast in understanding between those who know someone belongs to them and those who deny shared membership. One parent speaks

* In presenting and discussing examples, we refer to people by their first names. This is because people have different concerns about confidentiality. Some people would be happy to be known by their full real name, others prefer not to be so identified, others have already acquired pseudonyms from other authors. We have chosen to treat people equally by using only first names. We hope that this will not seem disrespectful.

for many who resist professional pressure to set someone outside their membership,

> *"The doctors told us he would never learn anything or be anything. They said, 'Put him away and forget him.' But he was ours, so we ignored them and took him home. They said he'd never roll over, but he can walk. They said he'd never talk, but he has even learned to read a little. They said he'd never feed himself, but now he has a job in a restaurant. They said he'd be a burden, but it's people like them, who still don't see his humanity, that burden us most. Why can't people welcome him for who he is?"* (O'Brien, 1988)

Setting some people apart may be one of humanity's most common boundary defining mechanisms.* Groups can say who they think they are by contrasting themselves favorably with inferior outsiders. Groups can define their rules of conduct by pointing at the immoral or outlandish customs of foreigners. Groups can generate strong feelings of closeness and common purpose by defining an enemy whose otherness is terrible and menacing. Groups can defend individual members from frightening impulses by projecting the unacceptable onto outsiders. In each case, the identity of an us depends on maintaining a depersonalized them.

But why should disability create a *them*? Michael was born among people with a strong sense of us, but he became one of them, even to most members of his family. How does his learning difficulty lead to a common sense that he is not one of our kind but someone who will be happiest apart from us, with his own kind?

Why can't some people recognize disabled people as belonging to them? When citizens of a community shaped by the moral exclusion of people with disabilities stop to think about it at all, they justify exclusion variously: people with disabilities have incurable sicknesses requiring continuous special treatment; they are dangerous to ordinary people or threatened by ordinary people's insensitivity; people with disabilities lack full humanity because of missing abilities and defective sensibilities.

Whatever the reason, those morally excluded as "not one of us" live outside the boundary within which positive values and ordinary considerations of fairness apply. At its historic extreme, moral exclusion led to systematic killing as a legally and professionally sanctioned medical treatment of people with severe disabilities (Gallagher, 1989).

In its everyday reality, denial of membership decreases severely disabled people's power to pursue their own goals and increases

*For a helpful general discussion of the causes and consequences of moral exclusion, see Opotow (1990).

their vulnerability to dehumanizing, or neglectful, or abusive treatment. Sometimes predators victimize people with disabilities, but people who mean well can also diminish excluded people's humanity. As Connie Marteniz (1988) says of her experience,

> *"So when I was growing up everybody either thought they had to take care of me, like my parents and my brothers and sisters, or they pushed me away, like some of my relatives and most of my teachers who stuck me out of the way...*
>
> *My parents always had a dream for my brothers and sisters for when they grew up, but nobody ever had a dream for me, so I never had a dream for myself...*
>
> *Quality of life would make a mother support her daughter [in having and pursuing a dream]. That is very important. In my case, there was not support. When I was a child, the doctor said to my parents: 'You may have a dream for a perfect child, but forget about that. The case is you parented a broken child.' And that was Connie."* (p. 1-2)

When professional service providers set up a program to assist morally excluded people, they often mindlessly follow this recipe: group outsiders together, set them physically apart, isolate them socially, amplify stigma and arouse a sense of differentness, control the details of their lives (often in the name of therapy), enforce material poverty as a condition of assistance, offer relatively greater benefits to those clients who seem more like "one of us" and less to those apparently less familiar, and expect obedience and gratitude in return.

Though institutional settings typically express this pattern of denied membership, service reforms often do too.

John Lord and Alison Pedlar (1990) conducted a follow-up study of the quality of everyday life for 18 of the 260 people moved into small community group homes as the Government of British Columbia closed its institution at Tranquille. Like about 40% of the people deinstitutionalized by this initiative, these 18 people all have some continuing contact with at least one family member. Four years after moving, eight people have only one person apart from paid staff in their social network; the other ten people have two or three people in their social network. Typically these network members are family and former staff: family members, usually parents, remain people's most frequent contacts (they visit 14 of the people at least once a month) and five people have a friend among present or former staff members. One person knows a community member who was recruited to befriend him; one person's sister has actively included him in her network of activities and relationships; and one person is an active member of her church. People's most common roles outside their group homes and day programs are those of consumer and spectator: two or three times a week they visit restaurants and shops or movie theaters or bowling lanes, usually as one among a group of people with disabilities. Of the 18 different four person group homes people live in, only six homes enable resident participation in daily routines and actively support positive relationships among housemates. In eight homes, people seem incompatible with one another and there is continuing tension or overt conflict between residents. Staff in a majority of homes spend most of their time either disengaged from residents or vigilantly monitoring and managing people's movements.

Margaret Flynn (1989) interviewed adults with mental retardation who receive some human service program assistance to live in their own apartments. Though almost all 88 people strongly prefer living independently to more supervised alternatives, she identifies 29 people who have been victimized in one or more ways, including: having money taken (17 people), being verbally intimidated by adults living nearby (15 people), having property damaged (12 people), and being mugged (2 people). She associates victimization with two human service program practices: channeling vulnerable people into undesirable neighborhoods and housing sites characterized as 'hard to rent', and failing to provide relevant training and support in presenting and standing up for one's self.

Summarizing his investigation of one region's implementation of supported employment, David Hagner (1989) reports that the alternative resembles the programs it was intended to reform. By observation and interview, he compared the experiences of non-disabled workers with the experiences of disabled people placed by a supported employment program. When performing the same jobs that human service staff choose for disabled workers to do, non-disabled employees regard those jobs as undesirable, temporary, and low status; non-disabled workers distance themselves from the job with such justifications as, "I'm only doing this temporarily." Non-disabled people do tasks in different ways than their disabled co-workers do because, usually for their own convenience, human service staff modify the ways disabled workers perform tasks: disabled people's jobs are "structured to an inordinate degree, almost fossilized, into an invariant sequence of tasks" (p. 85). Supervisors and co-workers express acceptance and approval of disabled workers, but regardless of this, job coaches attend to picking out and trying to remediate disabled employees' deficiencies and incapacities. Despite frequent, positive interactions among non-disabled workers at job sites, none of the supported employees participate much in these exchanges or form close working relationships because job coaches schedule the disabled worker's arrival, break and work time differently from those of their co-workers and because job coaches frequently insert themselves between workers with disabilities and their co-workers as buffers or interpreters.

A new program design won't make a significant difference until the people who plan it and the people who implement it confront their own program's potential to change all the details and still leave people with disabilities excluded from the circle of membership.

Unless people with severe disabilities, their allies, and those who serve them continuously widen their common recognition as members, the negative effects of moral exclusion will continue to undermine the quality of community life. Knowing another person as a member doesn't necessarily lead to treating the other person right, but such knowledge forms the foundation for civil and supportive relationships. Understanding that another person belongs to us doesn't necessarily disclose what to do when conflicts or difficulties arise, but such knowledge motivates action to strengthen common bonds rather than to ignore or sever them.

Recognition of membership grows as more and more people share the everyday experiences of schooling, working, playing, neighborhood living, and citizenship alongside people with severe disabilities in ways that highlight and strengthen the knowledge that we are all members of one another.

Known as a member

Jean and David are friends. In a book they wrote together, David writes about his life and they each talk about their friendship. In her account, Jean says, *"One Saturday David rode the bus over to see me and to see if there was anything he could do to help me. My mother had been bedridden for two years and I had been caring for her at home. There had been many difficult days but now she had pneumonia and there seemed to be no way she could fight it off. David stood beside her bed with me and spoke:*

"I am sorry you are hurting."

As he put his left arm around me and took my mother's hand in his right hand, he said what I really wanted to hear:

"It's OK to cry."

And we all three stood there and cried." (48) (Edwards & Dawson, 1983)

George attends a sheltered workshop. He lived in an institution, then in a group home, and now in an apartment. Based on his interest in bingo and with Bob's sponsorship, George became an active member of the Knights of Columbus. Over the three years of his membership, George has become more outgoing as he participates in a wide variety of activities, including working with his brother knights to run weekly bingo games. Recently George used his lodge contacts to become the top fund raiser for another local organization he is interested in. (Osburn, 1988; LaFrancis, 1990)

After 14 years in a sheltered workshop, a friend helped Kitty find a part time office job where she met and then became friends with Shirley. Kitty and Shirley frequently eat lunch together, and Kitty spends time with Shirley in Shirley's home. Shirley has helped Kitty expand her skills, take on additional job duties, increase her hours at work, and take a community college course. She says, *"[Kitty) is so eager to learn that I get excited showing her things... I get a lift out of that."* (9)

Shirley sees helping Kitty to improve her work performance as part of their friendship. *"I have taken it upon myself to worry about her as far as her livelihood... say if something happens to her parents... having her skills so that she could eventually go out and get a full time job and not having to rely as much as she does on other people... it's just something that I think about and I think that's one of the reasons I'm motivated to show her different things...* (11) (Lutfiyya, 1990)

The varieties of social support

Social support* is a convenient but abstract term which summarizes the effects of what people do for one another naturally, through everyday exchange of acknowledgment, information, emotion, and help. In discussing social support, some writers focus on immediate and specific results, such as help moving into a new apartment or consolation in time of grief. Others emphasize the cumulative effects of supportive ties on an overall sense of well being and health.

Passing the time of day with another person contributes to social support. Telling an acquaintance about a job opening contributes to social support. Listening to a friend as he struggles with a disappointment contributes to social support. Bringing in a vacationing neighbor's mail contributes to social support. Loaning a ladder to a friend contributes to social support. Running an errand contributes to social support. Bringing food to a wake contributes to social support. Helping a co-worker figure out a new task contributes to social support. Taking in a friend who has left her home contributes to social support. Hosting a celebration of a co-worker's achievement contributes to social support. Sharing a day at the beach contributes to social support. Visiting someone who is sick contributes to social support.

And, because the benefits of social support result from interaction, receiving each of these contributions also increases social

* Some people use other terms like natural support, natural help, or community caring with a similar meaning. We generally refer to social support with the intention of including these other terms.

support. In the enactment of shared membership, receiving assistance means as much as offering it.

These personal exchanges occur routinely and, if asked, the people involved usually explain them by reference to their understanding of the relationship they share. Thus, David says that consoling Jean and her mother is part of being a friend, Shirley teaches and encourages Kitty because of her friendship, and Bob would probably explain his contribution to George's favorite charity as a consequence of their fraternal relationship. Social support can mean mobilizing substantial resources to help another through a crisis, but much social support manifests itself in actions that happen in such small, familiar ways that people don't notice them and even find it odd when someone calls attention to them (Leatham & Duck, 1990).

Social support arises from at least four distinct experiences; thus people weave their memberships with four different threads.

- Feeling attached to emotionally important other people
- Having the opportunity to engage in shared activities
- Being part of a network of people who can approach one another for information and assistance
- Having a place and playing a variety of roles in economic and civic life.

Each of these four social resources contributes distinctly to well being, and one resource won't substitute for the others (Weiss, 1973). An active person may still feel deep emotional loneliness. A person with deep attachments may lack the connections to make personally important changes. But in combination of its forms, the quantity and quality of social support makes a demonstrable difference to health, to longevity, to the sense of satisfaction with life, and to personal and social power and effectiveness (House, Umberson, & Landis, 1988; Pilisuk & Parks, 1986).

Part of what we know about distinguishing the variety of social supports comes from the different personal consequences of experiencing their absence (Weiss, 1982). When we miss important attachments with intimates, we feel the pain of emotional loneliness. When we lack opportunities for participation with friends, we endure the boredom, aimlessness, and marginality of social isolation. When we are outside a network of personal contacts, we are disadvantaged by insufficient information and limited access to people with resources important to our purposes. Without positive roles in economic and associational life, we have a constrained sense of who we are and diminished power to discover and accomplish what we desire.

Social support counts as much for civic as for personal life. Anastasia Shkilnyk (1985) chronicles the near destruction of a community in her history of the Ojibwa people of Grassy Narrows, Ontario. She describes the vicious circle that begins turning when economic exploitation and physical dislocation combine with inept government assistance policies to break the ties and connections of everyday life. In the resulting vortex of violence, addiction, and cynicism, a people can lose their capacity to raise their children, make their livings, assist their elders, and govern themselves. Less dramatically but as importantly, a growing literature defines the fundamental social importance of altruism – acting with the intention to benefit another person- and the civic challenge of developing ways that people can express their sense of care for one another (Kahn, 1990; Piliavin & Charng, 1990).

Controversies around social support

While almost no one disagrees about the desirability of the actions summed up as social support, citizens should vigorously discuss its implications for public policy. Three characteristics of social support as a concept hinder this necessary debate. Because it is an abstraction which includes a wide variety of everyday behaviors, those who want to talk about social support have a hard time knowing exactly what it means. Indeed, Benjamin Gottlieb (1988) reports that a meeting of researchers on social support, convened by the US National Institute of Mental Health to agree on specific criteria for its definition, only made progress in their discussions when they stopped trying to define social support. Because it is by definition a good thing, those who want to debate social support have trouble raising questions about its limits and problems without sounding sour and cynical. Because it is a technical term, often used as if it described the raw material of professional intervention, citizens may have trouble finding a place in the discussion.

Unless citizens exercise caution, the concept of social support will obscure a necessary fact about the foundations of civil life. We will forget that we are members of each other and that the quality of our lives depends on our remembering this in daily action. To learn more about social support, let particular situations test general claims. This newspaper description of John and Marie's situation opens a window into some important controversies around social support.

While we have not met John and his family, we discuss their situation because it provides the human dimension in a special report by a major newspaper. We think the writer purposely selected a "good" family -long married parents in their own suburban home with two other grown, successful children- in order to influence public policy by showing the human costs of a scarcity of facilities. The newspaper writer advocates increasing the stock of group homes and assumes that sufficient public funding in a time of deficit is the only point at issue. We will read her account of John's family for what we can learn about social support.

John, 31, lives with his mother and father and attends a day activity program. He relies on his 73 year old mother, Marie, to assist him with bathing, going to the toilet, and with his meals. She says, *"My other kids have gone off, but because of John, I've never had that empty house feeling_ Between my four kids, I've been taking care of children for 48 years, and the most time I've had off was one week."*

Her fear is that she will die before John is settled in a group home. She says she doesn't expect her other children to look after John, *"Johnny is my problem, and you never really know how your daughter's husband or your son's wife would feel about taking care of him. They'd do it if they had to... But they have their own kids, and they're so busy... A permanent thing wouldn't be fair to them."* (13) (Lewin, 1990)

Should we say that John's mother provides "natural support"?

Beyond making a home for John and sharing her daily life with him, John's mother, Marie, organizes her day, as she has organized almost half her life time, around the physical work of taking care of him. She also cares about him: she loves her son and feels anxious about his future. This concern leads her to advocate for more group homes and for John's admission to one of them. Policy makers might sweep these different types of caring together under headings like "natural support" or "care by the community" and briefly admire Marie for kindly giving up her time to look after her son. A common, often unspoken, assumption that such caring is a family responsibility and that within the family caring is naturally part of a woman's place makes such a sweeping together easier (Traustadottir, 1990; Ungerson, 1987).

The newspaper story reflects this sexist assumption with a twist on the stereotypical portrayal of the silent wife whose picture adds interest to her husband's story. John's father lives with John and Marie and is pictured with them in a large photograph accompanying the article. However, he does not speak in the article, which refers to him only once:

"The specter (of Marie's dying before John moves to a group home) took on new immediacy this month after she passed out briefly in the bathroom and her husband went to pieces. 'He panics too easily,' she said. 'I'm not sure he could handle Johnny without me.'" (p 13)

Calling Marie's work natural support may be accurate, but misleading. Speaking of Marie's contribution in the same breath as the contribution of a neighbor who might occasionally share an afternoon with John hides a fundamental fact. The whole visible system of residences and day programs for people with mental retardation floats on the invisible work that Marie and tens of thousands of other women do every day. A recent US survey of the need for personal assistance among all people over 15 years of age identifies relatives as providing most of the assistance people require. Relatives are the sole source of assistance for 74% of people who need assistance with personal care, for 71% of people who need assistance with mobility, and for 67% of people who need assistance with household work (World Institute on Disability & Rutgers University Bureau of Economic Research, n.d.). Without Marie's work, unaccounted in cash and thus considered economically unproductive, the service system would face a fiscal crisis that pales its current substantial shortfalls. But because policy makers overlook her contribution, dismissing it as the proper feminine response to a private family trouble, her concerns get left out of decisions about taxation and public spending (Finch, 1989).

Even facts about obvious demographic changes influence policy discussion only marginally. Most everyone knows that a rising proportion of women work outside their homes, and many people know that a growing number of them now provide a substantial part of the practical care and economic support for their elders as well as for their children. Policy makers often rehearse these facts as if to exorcise them by repetition rather than to soberly consider their implications. Citizens can't allow the concept of social support to hide the amount of real work it takes to raise children and honorably assist elders and those of us with disabilities. Instead of allowing professionals to offer answers in the form of confusing generalizations about natural support, citizens should insist on focused discussion of the ways public policy and service practices affect how family members care for one another and how people isolated from family and friends will find informal support (Walker, 1986).

Can John depend on natural support for his future?

Marie sees two options for John: live with one of her other children or live in a publicly funded residence. She wants to reject the first option as unfair to her non-disabled children and her grandchildren, but fears that the slow pace of growth in residential services may leave her children no choice but to take him in or to place him in an institution (if that is even possible). She notes the irony in the fact that if she had followed professional advice to institutionalize John when he was an infant, he would now have a much better chance to be placed in a group home. By saving the state much of the cost of care for John, she has left the state in a position to ignore him. She does not speak about the possibility that she herself -like many older people- will face institutionalization if she becomes infirm unless her daughter or her daughter-in-law offers substantial practical assistance.

One can understand, though not excuse, policy makers ignoring John and the thousands of other disabled adults now living with their parents. When pressed, responsible officials justify ignoring John with complaints about tight budgets and reference to mixed signals about public willingness to cut other expenditures or pay more taxes so that John has more options. They assign responsibility to shortcomings at other levels of government or to insufficient efforts by charitable organizations. They call these excuses practical realities.

This sense of practical reality includes unquestioned individualism at its foundation. From this perspective, John, whose bad luck with his genetic endowment creates a private problem for his family, has had good luck because his parents have taken care of him and his government offers him a day program. When his family will no longer care for him, his luck will go bad and he will have to accept whatever he gets. As long as his mother continues to look after him uncomplainingly, she is upholding family values. But if she seeks help, especially help at home under her own control, conflict begins. Some policy makers oppose offering more than small amounts of help because they think such intervention erodes what they call family values. Other professional decision makers want to insure that getting help is difficult in order to control what they insensitively call the woodwork effect. (They mean that effective services would draw people in need "out of the woodwork.")

If defining John as the victim of bad luck seems unhelpful, consider the most common alternative explanation. This way of explaining disability assumes that ours is a just world in which people get what they deserve. From this perspective, John or his family somehow deserve visitation with private tragedy in retribution for something they did wrong.

Whether people use misfortune or misconduct to explain John's condition, the implication remains: John's private troubles set him and his family apart from us. We may, if we choose, respond with whatever pity and material charity we can manage. But he and his situation make no moral claim on us. This distance shapes law. No US court has yet held that John has an enforceable right to the service he requires, and even the most progressive legislatures have not gone beyond granting him the privilege of professional screening and placement on a waiting list.

Neither of Marie's apparent options look promising for her and John. Is there another way? Some concerned people combine their frustration at the cold clumsiness of service bureaucracies with their belief in people's willingness to help one another out. They suggest that natural support offers John and his parents -and perhaps overburdened government- a third alternative. Under what conditions could that be true?

If a wider group of people recognized John's membership with them, he would have more people who like and care about him. He would probably have more social resources to draw upon. Presently, his life appears constrained between his membership in his parent's family and clienthood in a day program that walls him off from the ordinary relationships of community life. If one or another of John's personal interests led to his belonging to a community association, he would probably have a more varied and interesting weekly schedule and he might have more allies to work for changes that will benefit him. If John invested some of his energy with members of available social networks, more information and everyday assistance would probably come his way, as it probably would if his family invested energy and made requests on his behalf. If John's neighbors recognized him as belonging among them, he would probably be able to call on a variety of kinds of everyday help and support, especially in clear emergencies which call for straightforward, time limited help. If members of John's extended family accept and enjoy him as a family member, he probably has a claim on a share of whatever resources the rest of the family has. If John had close friends, he would probably have more personal support and encouragement, and, to the extent of his friends' resources, he might be able to draw on more social influence and material goods.

These social resources, available more or less spontaneously and voluntarily once people endorse his membership with them, would greatly improve his possibilities for enjoying a good life. However, three problems cloud John's prospects. The first problem arises from John's current social isolation. The second two problems arise from the social norms that channel the kind and extent of help people will typically offer someone they recognize as belonging to them (Willmott, 1987).

First, though some people do spontaneously reach out to include people whose disabilities significantly inhibit their mobility and communication, moving from isolation to membership typically takes hard work. Very few available services focus on increasing social involvement and most programs actively separate people with walls. Therefore, many of the people with severe disabilities who enjoy membership in community networks and associations do so because their parents -most often their mothers- refused to accept their isolation and worked hard to overcome it. Anyone who would blame John's parents for his isolation and exhort them to work harder to integrate him should contemplate the biblical judgement on those who put together heavy burdens for others to carry (*Matthew*, 23, 2-4).

Second, though some people do spontaneously make heroic efforts for friends and neighbors, John's social world is shaped by rules which express the premise that each person has the individual ability to deal with everyday responsibilities in the long run. Thus, people will offer friends and neighbors and co-workers extraordinary help to see them through a bad time or to aid recovery from a crisis. Those who help may not expect repayment from those they assist, but they typically expect them to recover and get on with their lives in a reasonable period of time. John violates this common expectation of recovery. Even if good instruction and better assistive technology greatly improve his ability to manage his daily routine and contribute productively to economic life, John will most likely need some assistance and guidance and protection throughout the day, everyday, for the rest of his life.

The strength of the expectation that extraordinary help will be somehow time limited shows in the concern and confusion some adoptive families of severely disabled children experience as their children grow up and they confront Marie's dilemma. They entered the adoption freely, and they share their family life generously, but as they realize the lack of acceptable alternative living arrangements they experience anger with the human service system and sometimes resentment of their disabled adult son or daughter for violating the expectation that their family relationship would change as their son or daughter grew up and moved out.

The enduring everydayness of severely disabled people's need for assistance constitutes a strain on them and the people who love them. As Judith Snow (1990), a physically disabled teacher and activist says,

> *"The hardest part for me is that, no matter what mood I wake up in, the biggest thing on my agenda everyday is to support my attendants and supporters."*

Third, John needs types of assistance which seem unusual to most people because of their intimacy. A friend who accompanies him on an overnight trip will have to deal with helping him use the toilet and take a bath. A co-worker who wants to show him a better way to do his job will have to account for his limited communication and learning skills. A guardian will have to continuously maintain balance between imposing choices on John and seeking and respecting his preferences. None of these kinds of assistance lie beyond most people's competence, and many people who willingly provide them say they are "no big deal." But they lie far enough outside the typical ways that people exchange help to create a barrier. Marie may experience this barrier as a sense that it's too much to ask others to accommodate John's needs. Another person, who might be willing to assist if asked, may be inhibited by discomfort, by a fear of intruding, and by deference to the assumed superiority of those professionals who deal with needs that appear unusual.

It seems reasonable to believe that John could rely on people and associations who know him as a member for many opportunities and for a wide range of kinds of assistance. However, unless people make a conscious and sustained effort to create new ways to organize the expression of their care for one another, the conclusion of Peter Willmott's (1986) review of the literature on available natural support probably holds. He writes,

> *"Families with children or other members [with severe disabilities] may not be socially isolated, but they are likely to lack informal support of a sustained kind from outside the household." (p. 79)*

The chances that people outside his family will spontaneously come forward to offer John a lifelong home with them are slim enough to make it unfair to John and his family to build policy on that (implicit) expectation. And it is unjust to leave John no option but to accept others' charity, no matter how generously given, for such fundamentals as his home and a chance to work.

How do human service programs influence the social support John experiences?

If John moves from his parent's home into a professionally directed, government funded group home, he becomes a service client 24 hours of every day. His schedule, his movements, his activities, and his contacts with other people come under the full time scrutiny and control of an interdisciplinary team of human service professionals and their para-professional agents.

What effects can this status have on other citizen's active recognition of his membership in them? On the basis of a national survey of US community residences for people with mental retardation, Bradley Hill and his associates (1984) report that about eight out of ten residents have no regular social contact with non-disabled people. In an evaluation of the effects of a national policy aimed at improving community care for people with mental retardation, Gerry Evans and Ann Murcott (1990) show that almost half the people who use services in four different Welsh communities have no close friends at all and less than one person in four has any friend who is not also a client in the same service. In a pointed reflection on his visit to a community group home, McKnight (1989a) says,

> *"...if one would say to the average citizen, 'I want you to take five men and buy a house in a neighborhood in a little town where those five men can live for ten years. And then I want you to be sure that they are unrelated in any significant way to their neighbors, that they will have no friends, and that they will be involved in none of the associational or social life of the town.,' I think that almost every citizen would say that this is an impossible task.*
>
> *Nonetheless... systems of ...community services have managed to achieve what most citizens would believe impossible - the isolation of labeled people from community life even though they are embedded in a typical house in a friendly neighborhood in an average town." (2)*

Some policy analysts see an obvious answer to the isolation and cost created by most current services. Simply combine professionally controlled services (which they often call formal support) with informal or natural support. In this perspective, service workers (often called case managers) make up packages of formal and informal care which match individual needs. Their work will succeed because of their presumed professional skill at assessing and assisting natural supporters. Professionals will multiply the resources available to John while reducing the cash price of his assistance. They will do so by recruiting volunteer companions for isolated people, and by setting up and advising self-help groups, and by organizing the contribution of natural helpers (as professionals have called those people whom others seek out for advice and assistance).

Three problems complicate implementation of this obvious answer. First, something like the informal supports these analysts describe exist all right, but not necessarily in a form that makes them easily identified or coordinated or delivered on schedule in professionally defined doses. What professionals call natural support relationships are necessarily unpredictable. Predictably this stimulates scholarly discussion of how to decide when informal supporters behave inappropriately and what to do about it (Coyne, Wortman, & Lehman, 1988).

Second, many citizens resist attempts to treat them as human service extenders. Co-workers who voluntarily give aid and acceptance to a fellow employee with a disability balk at being seen as part of the person's treatment team, especially when a case manager the co-worker has never met claims to be captain of the team. Some people that professionals identify as part of a person's natural support system say that it becomes harder to be with a person they care about when they are expected to adopt a professional attitude toward their friend.

Third, it is by no means certain that an adequate number of people have time and energy to match the extent of need. As Alan Walker observes (1982), a government that expects a community to care is guilty of cynicism if it fails to make substantial investments in developing and maintaining an adequate context for caring. In economically developed places, this context includes affordable housing, a fair income, efficient transportation for people who don't have cars, access to decent health care, reasonable child care options, and working conditions that make room for the work of caring and civic participation without exhausting workers. Many Americans live and support one another admirably without these conditions in place. But any weaknesses in the social context decrease the time and energy community members have for John.

If no simple recipe easily blends formal and natural support, does John have an alternative to relying solely on the support of his family, or trusting in the spontaneous support of other community members, or becoming a full time client in isolation? Beyond insuring a social context for mutual caring, can public funds enable ways to combine the resources in John's family and community to support him to live in dignity and safety as a recognized member?

Some thoughtful critics give very long odds on a positive answer to this question. Ivan Illich argues (1976) that increased human ability to analyze life into technically defined problems and hierarchically administered solutions inevitably yields ironic results. With each new possibility for individual expression comes an equal possibility for expanded domination. For example, our desire for medical relief from pain binds us to engineered solutions that erode our ability to care for one another in times of suffering. Healing turns from counsel on living with suffering and dying well to medical control of both the person and a rising share of common wealth in the name of cure. As physicians encounter maladies for which they have no engineered solution, they push for even greater professional control with the result that people's capacity to care and suffer declines even more. This bind generates specifically counterproductive outcomes: more investment in technical solutions creates less health and more impersonal domination of human life.

Extending Illich's analysis to the situation of people with developmental disabilities, John McKnight (1989a, 1989b) identifies a trade off between service and community. The more investment in services, the less community capacity can exist. From this perspective, human service workers steal people with disabilities away from community, and with them the community's capacity for care. Services enrich their workers at the expense of cash income for the people they serve. Service worker's activities systematically dominate and erode ordinary people's capacity to care. Community capacity will flourish when professional dominance is broken and the cash invested directly in services is redistributed to the people who are now clients.

McKnight links his vision of community members with untapped capacity for care to his exposure of professional services as the corrosive agent responsible for isolating disabled people and weakening their fellow citizen's ability to care. His argument deserves to be questioned. Addiction to inflating assets by manipulating financial instruments rather than by making useful things may be at least as erosive of community as social work is. Elected representatives may not be so easily bamboozled by professional rhetoric as McKnight implies: they may vote appropriations for professional services because they want to exclude and control people whose common membership they deny. And those people who reject disabled people as neighbors and co-workers and schoolmates may not just be victims of professional manipulation or ineptitude. Some of them may indeed fear and blindly despise people they experience as other. But beyond thoughtful debate, McKnight's argument merits testing in action. Can John establish membership in the networks and associations available to his non-disabled brother and sister? How can public resources be re-directed in ways that build community settings which include and support John?

A Fertile Dilemma

So John and those who want to help him face a dilemma. Well intentioned efforts to service him are likely to destroy his chances of shared membership and weaken the fabric of ordinary relationships necessary to support every member of his community. But up to now the spontaneous responses of John's community have left him isolated within his family and quite unlikely to find a home and a chance for meaningful activity without organized and (probably) paid for assistance.

This dilemma points to fertile, but stony, ground for people who want to create new social forms. Those people who are potential resources to John need organized ways to recognize his membership with them. They are poorer without him. And John needs reliable assistance that supports his belonging. He is vulnerable without it. How can people committed to recognizing his membership weave a more subtle web with John and his fellow citizens?

A small but growing number of innovators accept this dilemma. Sobered by the possibility that their well intentioned efforts might undermine the community of their desires, and uncertain of who will come forward to recognize and provide daily assistance to people whose membership is in doubt, they work to build new relationships and better forms of assistance. An account of the early news from along several of their paths forms the rest of this chapter.

Building community by expanding membership

Three emerging social forms, invented specifically to establish recognition of disabled people as community members, share a common vision and common basic assumptions. Their practitioners work to build communities in which disability does not threaten membership, communities in which disabled people have real opportunities and obligations to discover and contribute their personal gifts. Their practitioners believe:

- Many if not most people with severe disabilities are vulnerable to exclusion and isolation unless someone makes a focused effort to establish and support their membership
- Because of the oppression of prejudice and isolation, many severely disabled people and their families face substantial barriers to making connections on their own behalf
- Many people who are already members of community networks and associations will include people with severe disabilities in their lives and activities given an opportunity to do so
- Once people who have been separated by apparent disability recognize their common membership, many form mutually satisfying relationships despite apparent differences in ability, appearance, and lifestyle
- The social fact of exclusion on the basis of disability, routinely expressed in patterns of everyday life and reinforced by most social policies and service practices, makes it a political act to pursue relationships that contradict exclusion
- The work of expanding community membership is different from almost every existing form of service to people with disabilities and needs to proceed independent of usual systems
- Increasing community inclusiveness benefits all people, not just people with disabilities.

These beliefs lead to conscious efforts to redefine the boundaries of shared membership by learning new ways of assisting disabled people to take their place in community.

Each of these three social inventions takes a different path. One builds up community by assisting people to develop personal relationships. Another expands connections to community associations. The third helps people to create circles of support for the expression and pursuit of their dreams.

While each path is distinct, those who successfully practice each form of community building share fundamental approaches to bridging the social distance created by exclusion. They find concrete ways to help people feel their membership in each other by assisting them to identify and act on common interests, to see one another's individuality, and to break the social rules that exclude disabled people (Bogdan & Taylor, 1989; Piliavin & Charng, 1990). They encourage shared activities that will help people become more comfortable with obvious differences (such as staff assigning pointless or infantile tasks as therapy or a person's unusual ways to communicate), deal constructively with practical consequences of disability (such as staff restricting a person from having visitors or a person's use of a wheelchair), and discover mutual satisfactions (such as shared delight in a good meal or pleasure in learning something new). And the paths cross one another. Common membership in a community association can lead to friendship. Members of a support circle may sponsor one another's membership in new associations. A strong and responsible personal relationship may form the nucleus of a support circle.

Citizen Advocacy

Michael moved from an institution to a group home and then to a "semi-independent living program," which he quit after meeting and marrying Heather, another person served by a service program. When Michael inherited some money, he agreed to let a local mental retardation agency manage it for him. Rather than protect and invest Michael's inheritance, agency staff spent his funds on everyday expenses in order to impoverish Michael and Heather so they would again qualify for federal income support.

AJ, who works as a citizen advocacy coordinator, agreed with Michael and Heather that he would find someone who would advocate to improve their financial situation. AJ approached Dennis, a prominent local accountant, and invited him to assist Michael.

Dennis voluntarily accepted responsibility to understand and represent Michael's interests as though they were his own. This commitment brought him into an extended conflict when he decided that the agency had irresponsibly mismanaged Michael's funds and should compensate Michael for their poor performance. Ultimately, Michael and Dennis were unsuccessful in recovering any of the mismanaged money. But Dennis did assist Michael to gain control of his remaining money, settle outstanding bills, adjust his lifestyle to live within his diminished income, and reinstate his benefits. He helped Michael find a stronger voice for himself by talking over Michael's options with him and supporting his considered choices. And, when Michael said he didn't want any more of Dennis's help, Dennis withdrew with an understanding that Michael could call on him again for help if he needed it. (Hildebrand, 1991)

Bridget and Harmony are mother and daughter. Two years ago, Harmony received homebound instruction because of her cerebral palsy and multiple hospitalizations for treatment of other neurological problems. Bridget's plans to start a support group for parents of disabled children failed because holding things together for Harmony took all of her available energy. In the process of trying to set up the support group, she met the two citizen advocacy coordinators, who agreed to recruit a citizen advocate for Harmony.

Colleen, who lives nearby, met Bridget and Harmony at the citizen advocacy coordinators' invitation. Colleen spends time with Harmony and enjoys Harmony's company. This not only gives Bridget regular time for other activities, it confirms Bridget's sense of her daughter as a person with important gifts to contribute.

As Colleen came to know and care for Harmony she became aware that Harmony had much to offer other people and decided that Harmony could learn, grow, and contribute in a regular school class. She encouraged and supported Bridget to challenge the professional recommendation that Harmony attend a segregated school in a rehabilitation facility 45 minutes away. Together they persuaded the neighborhood school to accept and provide the necessary support to include Harmony in a regular class, where she and her classmates now do well together (Hildebrand, 1991).

Though they live in the same town and might have passed one another on the street, Michael and Dennis live in different worlds. Though they live close to one another and have children of similar ages, Bridget was so busy taking care of Harmony that she probably would not have had time to meet Colleen. And even if the two women did meet, Bridget might well have felt uncomfortable asking Colleen to regularly take Harmony home with her.

Citizen advocacy coordinators assist those who are unlikely to meet because of the social exclusion of disabled people. They perform effective introductions and offer continued support to personal relationships. They assist freely given relationships: Michael and Harmony are not clients of the citizen advocacy office; Dennis and Colleen are not volunteers to the citizen advocacy office. The citizen advocacy office, which must be independent of the service system, respects and supports the independence of the people in citizen advocacy relationships. A citizen advocacy coordinator focuses single-mindedly on building community by strengthening the bonds of membership between excluded people and ordinary citizens. Their ideal is a community in which more people recognize and act to promote another's human rights, concerns, and interests as if they were their own. Citizen advocacy coordinators want increasing numbers of people to live out one citizen advocate's words,

> *"I look at him like he was me. I put myself in his shoes, and then I help him out however I can."*

At their best, citizen advocacy relationships form a new kind of social space, a space in which people relieve one another of stereotypes, broaden one another's range of life experiences, and deepen one another's appreciation of what it means to belong. Dennis grew to respect Michael's independence and strength as he learned firsthand of the barriers put in Michael's way by an irresponsible, over controlling agency. Michael grew to respect and trust Dennis because Dennis listened to him first and then offered him practical help based on what Michael said. Colleen and Bridget have come to share a love and concern for Harmony that led them to action which has opened their neighborhood school to children with severe disabilities. Both Dennis and Colleen describe mutual relationships in which they gain (often in unexpected ways) as well as give. Many of the satisfactions of citizen advocacy relationships come from the small pleasures of being together, and getting to know another person, and discovering ways that someone whose life experiences have been very different shares similar feelings and concerns.

People choose a variety of ways to live out citizen advocacy relationships. Sometimes they simply spend time together, sometimes they seek a better response from service agencies, and sometimes they find ways to get what people need outside the service system. Michael and Dennis began their relationship around practical financial problems. They developed a friendly working relationship which expanded as Dennis helped Michael to make better money decisions and to represent his wishes to the operators of the sheltered workshop he attends. Once Michael had the degree of independence he wanted, he stopped regular contact with Dennis. Bridget and Harmony began their relationship with Colleen around Harmony's desire to do things with other people away from home and Bridget's need for some time to herself. From this beginning, they decided to confront their school system's decisions about Harmony. After their success, they continue to support one another day to day.

Like anyone who has an ally, disabled people in citizen advocacy relationships have added strength in dealing with threats and pursuing their interests. And citizen advocates often expand their partner's social network by including the disabled person in their own network of friends and associations. But having an ally, even a strong and loyal ally who shares many resources, doesn't guarantee that situations will come out right. Because of his relationship with Dennis, Michael has more control of his finances, but he has fewer resources because the agency that impoverished him evaded its responsibility to him. Dennis affirms Michael's desire for independence, even though that leads Michael to say no to his offers of further contact and help. The rewards of citizen advocacy relationships come more from a sense of doing the right thing together than from the assurance of good results. One person with a disability summarizes a long effort she and her partner have made to get her a suitable communication device,

> *"We haven't won yet. They're tough, but we're still trying to educate them. They keep beating us, but we hang in there."*

Andy Baxter (1991) studied the ways effective citizen advocacy coordinators do and think about their work. Beginning from a citizen advocacy coordinator's maxim, "all we have to work with is questions," he highlights the importance of a well focused question to guide the process of introducing people. A good question summarizes what the coordinator knows of the disabled person on whose behalf the coordinator seeks a partner. Powerful questions exactly focus the person's situation in terms clear enough that another citizen can respond with an active yes or a definite no. Much of the citizen advocacy coordinator's art grows from the ability to clearly frame and fearlessly pose such questions. Citizen advocacy coordinators have no recipe and no magic to guarantee a good question, but the search for better questions is at the heart of their work. Well focused questions take shape from intuitions which arise out of careful listening and disciplined thinking.

Sandy is a young woman who has lived briefly in several group homes, but has always been asked to leave after a short time and returned to her parents home. These experiences have left her feeling rejected. She does not work, refuses to attend a day time program, and acts in ways her parents see as irresponsible. Though she says she would like to leave her parents home and live more on her own, she has not been able to do so. Sandy says she would like a citizen advocate to be her friend and help her make it.

Elizabeth, the citizen advocacy coordinator, first considered following this question in her search for a partner for Sandy, "I am looking for a young woman, who lives nearby and has successfully left home. I will ask this person to be a guide and mentor for Sandy as she pursues her independence." But this way of framing the question didn't seem quite right. With more thought, Elizabeth saw that Sandy's life had been filled with people unsuccessfully giving guidance and advice and that her response to them was closely followed by their rejection of her. So the citizen advocacy coordinator's question shifted: "I am asking you to try to build a relationship with Sandy, in the hope that the two of you will come to like each other very much, and in the hope that yours will become a lasting, close friendship. Out of your friendship, gentle guidance can emerge, and you may not even realize that you are guiding your friend. Can you picture yourself as a person who can make a long, close, and faithful commitment to another person?" Based on this question, Elizabeth found Sandy a partner. (22) (Baxter, 1991)

Of course it will be up to Sandy and her partner to decide how their relationship goes. People give their relationships direction, shape, and texture as they respond to one another and to outside events over time. But the way citizen advocacy coordinators go about introducing people and supporting relationships makes an important difference to the quality of most relationships.

By introducing people one to another, citizen advocacy programs remind people of their shared membership in one another. By supporting relationships as they evolve, citizen advocacy programs strengthen people's ability to act responsibly toward one another.

Connecting People to Community Associations

Since her mother's death, Betty, who is in her 60's, had almost no contact with anyone outside the group home she lives in.

Then Betty met Kathy, who works on a community building project sponsored by the local neighborhood organization. From spending time with Betty, Kathy learned that Betty wanted to go to church, something she had enjoyed with her mother but lacked the opportunity to do.

Kathy asked Mary, a leader in the neighborhood association and a long time member of the Church of the Advent, to sponsor Betty's church membership. This means taking Betty to church every Sunday, sitting with her, and making sure she has opportunities to participate in the life of the congregation after formal services. Sometimes Mary, or someone else who knows Betty well, needs to "translate" for those church members who have difficulty understanding Betty.

Before the first Sunday, Mary was unsure that she would know what to do to assist Betty and uncertain whether she could spare the time to help Betty get to church. But her feelings changed, "*Once I met Betty, there was no way I could not take her to church. Betty's a neat person... she is enthusiastic and has a sense of humor. You don't have to put on any pretensions around her.*" (1)

Betty participates actively in services and particularly enjoys exchanging the greeting of peace with the rector and other members of the congregation. During the bishop's visitation, he processed through the church, blessing the people in each pew. When he blessed Mary and her family, Betty enthusiastically waved back to him. After the service, the bishop took time to meet Betty and spend a moment with her.

Betty saves each week's church bulletin. The bulletins are one small sign of her membership. They signify the only place where Betty belongs and is not one of a group of elderly, severely retarded clients. (LeWare, 1989)

As part of her job, Sharon developed community living arrangements in a small town for 8 people who had previously lived in nursing homes. As time went by, the pride she shared in their new homes turned into concern for their isolation. Her concern became confusion as she recognized that neither she nor her staff knew much about the life of the town and how to help outsiders become part of it.

Sharon enlisted Francis to act as a "bridge builder." Francis is a long-time leader of local associations from the town's marching band to a food pantry for the town's many unemployed industrial workers, She asked him, as an expert in community life, to introduce previously excluded people to community associations that will benefit from their contribution.

Francis introduced Arthur, a man who spent over 50 years in institutions, to membership in the core group of volunteers who operate the community food pantry. For more than 2 years, Arthur has greeted people as they arrive and handed them the numbers that tell them when it's their turn to be served. Though it can take Arthur a long time to complete a statement, his co-workers and a number of the people who come to the pantry say they enjoy talking to him.

Arthur's strong desire to help others forms the foundation of his membership. Because of their common desire, the other volunteers have overcome problems that some professionals identify as significant barriers to Arthur's community involvement. The other members of the core group have dealt with Arthur's inability to keep the number tags straight by teaching him to recognize more numbers and by helping him arrange the tags in order on a stick. The group's leader deals firmly with the few customers who occasionally complain about Arthur's presence. Rather than trying to correct him, the people at the food pantry have redefined his "institutional behavior" of securing possessions -such as his Food Pantry name tag- by wrapping them in multiple layers of handkerchiefs, old socks, and bags. His colleagues consider this habit Arthur's way of showing how much he prizes his name tag and how proud he is to belong with them. (Gretz, 1988).

Kathy and Sharon assisted Betty and Arthur to new roles in their community because they know their community differently than the residential and day staff who serve Betty and Arthur do. The staff see community as the location of their jobs, as the address of the buildings in which they provide residential and day activity services. For the staff, community includes places that staff might take Betty and Arthur if sufficient staff hours remain after providing state required treatments, and if the van is available, and if they are certain that Betty and Arthur have the skills to handle the requirements of the setting. Kathy and Sharon see community as a medium in which people join together to grow diverse associations. They are inspired by the late 20th century possibilities raised by Alexis de Tocqueville's (1990) observation on the distinctive character of early 19th century America.

> *Americans of all ages, all conditions, and all dispositions constantly form associations. They have not only commercial and manufacturing companies, ... but associations of a thousand other kinds, religious, moral, serious, futile, general or restricted, enormous or diminutive. (vol 2, p. 106)*

So Kathy and Sharon see the congregation of the Church of the Advent and the core group of the community food pantry. And they see Mary and Francis as able to welcome Betty and Arthur as members because Mary and Francis are already active members with a great potential to extend hospitality.

Arising along with their distinct perspective on community, Kathy and Sharon know Betty and Arthur in a different way than residential and day services staff do. Both Betty and Arthur are older and have numerous apparent disabilities. Because they have had limited success in remediation activities, staff see Betty and Arthur in terms of their deficits. Staff interpret Betty's and Arthur's disabilities as generalized limitations on the possibility that local people can accept them, except as full time service clients. Kathy and Sharon search for the personal interests and capacities that will connect Betty and Arthur to the associational life of their communities. John McKnight (1987) expresses the foundation for their confidence that Betty and Arthur belong,

> *"...community structures tend to proliferate until they create a place for everyone, no matter how fallible." (p. 3)*

For Kathy and Sharon, Betty and Arthur are not the problem. For them, the problem is Betty's and Arthur's disconnection from local associations. Kathy discovered the extent of this disconnection as she explored her neighborhood's associational life by interviewing over 100 of its leaders. Among these, the most active people in the neighborhood, only a few reported any contact at all with a severely disabled person, and none knew someone with a disability personally (O'Connell, 1990). These people, and the associations they lead, represent an untapped resource for people with severe disabilities. And people with severe disabilities can contribute new energy, new abilities, and new meaning to the associations that enliven the communities they live in. Kathy and Sharon choose to organize their work around discovering which of the many forms of local associational life suits Betty and Arthur and assisting them to join. They work through trust and time.

To discover opportunities, Kathy and Sharon identify community leaders, like Mary and Francis, and enlist their interest by appealing to the common value people place on hospitality. Thus, on behalf of outsiders, they gain an insider's knowledge of and access to a community's people and their associations. Francis sums up the art of involving people like this,

> *"To get people involved, you first have to let them know that they have something valuable to offer. Than you ask them. Period." (Gretz, 1991)*

Kathy and Sharon spend enough time with Betty and Arthur to appreciate them as individuals and to learn something of their gifts. Sometimes a person's interests are obvious. Arthur frequently says he wants to help people who are down on their luck. In this desire, Sharon can see a link between Arthur and Francis. Watching Betty pantomime kneeling and praying in church when asked what she likes to do leads Kathy to remember Mary's active role in her congregation. Sometimes, gifts are hidden and can only be discovered by people willing to thoughtfully share new experiences with a person.

To assist them to join an association that matches their interests, Kathy and Sharon encourage the association's members to reach out and include Betty and Arthur. Kathy and Sharon don't pose as disability inclusion experts, ready to solve every problem. They trust people's ability to find solutions for themselves once they recognize someone as a member. An association's capacity to create a place is especially strong when a well established member acts as the newcomer's sponsor, as Mary does for Betty and Francis does for Arthur. This trust in association members doesn't come easy. Sharon says,

> *...after Arthur had been at the pantry several months, Francis called me to say... that Arthur wasn't making it to the bathroom on time and was wetting himself. My reaction was one of horror and fear; fear that they were going to suggest he not come any more. Sure that I was going to beat Francis to the punch, I suggested perhaps someone else [from the residential program] could take Arthur's place.*
>
> *Francis was shocked. "Absolutely not!" he replied. Arthur belonged with them. They just wanted to solve the problem.* *(Gretz, 1991)*

Kathy and Sharon recognize that membership in a community association can bring new parts of a person to life. Arthur grows as his desire to help others finds an outlet that offers him responsibilities, challenges, and rewards. And they know that including someone previously outside the circle of membership can renew an association. Some members of Betty's congregation feel that her spontaneous responses -like hugging the people she knows best when it is time for the greeting of peace- bring their rituals back to their roots.

Bringing excluded people into membership satisfies and energizes their hosts, but not everyone extends a welcome. Mary O'Connell (1990) identifies four difficulties, rooted in people's lack of experience, that limit association member's readiness to include people with disabilities.

- Some people feel too busy to make time for a person who could require some extra assistance. Most active citizens balance work, family obligations, personal interests, and association duties and they may see including a person with a severe disability as a time consuming activity.
- People with severe disabilities raise some people's uncertainties about their competence to respond properly, the extent and limits of their responsibility, and their ability to deal with other's reactions to someone they assume is different. They don't see a disabled person as a potential contributor but as a kind of a project.
- Some association leaders think of involving people with severe disabilities as a kind of extra activity which competes with the group's mission and perhaps exposes the association to new liabilities.
- Some people plainly reject others with severe disabilities. And service providers often aggravate citizen concerns when they make it clear that they believe that "special" activities are better and that they ultimately control their clients' time.

New memberships significantly expand Betty's and Arthur's social worlds, but both people still spend most of their time as clients of human services because by nature the associations that welcome them don't offer more than part time involvement to any of their members. Their fellow members welcome them and accommodate their individual differences in the context of the church or the food pantry, and their membership may spill over into new acquaintances as growing numbers of people talk with Betty in the coffee hour after church or greet Arthur on the street. However, current service arrangements make their memberships fragile. The professional team that controls Betty's life could decide that she should move to a group home in another neighborhood. Direct service staff could discourage Arthur from spending time at the food pantry because it is too much bother for them to help him get ready. No doubt Mary and Francis would fight for Betty and Arthur's continuing membership, but the service programs retain power as long as Betty and Arthur remain tied to them by the lack of alternative sources of personal assistance. For now, Betty and Arthur's freedom of association depends on the value their service providers decide to place on their membership.

Kathy works in an inner city Chicago neighborhood. Sharon works in a small town hard hit by recession. Some people might doubt that either locality would have vital associations willing to welcome outsiders with severe disabilities. But, though troubled, both communities remain alive because some citizens invest their energy in building and sustaining associations. To find the associations that match the individual interests of people with severe disabilities requires that someone carefully follow leads from one person to the next in order to identify opportunities and sponsors. Both communities have associational leaders like Mary and Francis who will recognize and welcome the contribution of people with severe disabilities. To enlist them requires that someone earn their trust through an honest appeal to their sense of hospitality and a continuing willingness help with problem solving.

Kathy and Sharon confirm the importance of associations in community life by working to increase the diversity of people that association members recognize as belonging among their number. By so doing they strengthen their communities as they open new opportunities for people with severe disabilities.

Circles of Support

At 17, Kevin attended a segregated, hospital-based school for people with multiple handicaps. Because his teachers believed that he could not benefit from academic instruction, Kevin's educational program included physical therapy, music therapy, group therapy, and basic skills like shape and color identification, sorting, and collating. Because students in his class were collected from a large area, and because he went to school a long way from home, Kevin made few after school friendships. Despite his energy, his sense of humor, and his interests in sports, computers, and socializing, Kevin was isolated. Most of his contact was with his brother Jason, his mother, Linda, and his father, Carl.

Linda's concern for her son's future led her family into participation in a project aimed at developing circles of support. With the help of facilitators employed by the project, Linda invited two close friends and their teenagers and Tracy, a senior at the local high school who knew Kevin from summer camp, to meet in her home with her family. As the circle shared their appreciation of Kevin's capacities and ideas about his future, Jason challenged the circle to work for Kevin's inclusion in the local high school.

Kevin enthusiastically agreed, and the circle began several months of planning, problem solving, and advocacy with the school system. Some adult resource people joined the circle to help negotiate system problems. Some more students joined to help Kevin develop a schedule of classes and activities that matched his interests.

At 19, Kevin is a high school senior who particularly enjoys computer lab, art, history, and social science classes (where he completed a project on "Cerebral Palsy and the Brain"). In addition to attending school sports events, and social activities like the Prom, Kevin belongs to the Peer Leadership Club and the Future Business Leaders of America. His ability with the computer his circle helped him get has led him to join the local MacUsers group and his interest in graphic arts brought him membership in a local association of artists.

Kevin's circle continues to help him focus and work toward his vision of life after graduation. (Meadows, 1991)

Six years after graduating from college, Cathy was working part time as a writer and editor, and living with her mother, who provided most of the personal assistance she needed. Cathy says," an incredible sort of numb despair settled over my life" as she grappled with the barriers that surrounded her. She was unable to find a new living arrangement offering her the amount of attendant service she needs and couldn't break out of the benefits trap that keeps her from earning a fair wage. She stopped thinking about her future: "I would continue to live with my mother, working where and when I could, and when she co*uld no longer get me up and dressed and out of bed, I would go and live in a nursing home. I didn't like it, but I could see no other way."* (1988, p. 6)

Then Cathy saw a way to live "free and safe." In a workshop sponsored by a project exploring circles of support, she learned about cooperative housing associations and an approach to consumer controlled attendant services that could provide the assistance she needs to deal with her serious and continual breathing problems. She also got help in organizing her mother and 7 of her friends into a support circle.

Cathy's circle offers her encouragement, creative ideas, contacts, companionship, and practical help as she pursues her dream of a housing co-op. As she has worked over the past 3 years to make her dream real, the circle has grown to include a property developer and an expert on cooperatives. She and her circle have joined other activists to analyze and lobby for change in the policies that block decent housing and effective attendant services.

As she has pursued her big dream, Cathy has learned to realize smaller ones. With the support of her circle she has become more confident in hiring her own personal care assistants and more willing to travel and pursue new experiences. (Ludlum, 1991; 1988)

Kevin and Cathy and their circles of support demonstrate the possibilities of conscious interdependence. Before their circles formed, both lived as valued members of their families and both were service clients. However, without their circles, neither had the support to bring a vision of a desirable personal future into clear focus and neither had the social resources to work toward significant change in the way human services treat them.

Circles of support organize around dreams that have gone unheard, even by the person at the center of the circle. These dreams direct action because they communicate a person's unique capacities and gifts and thus define the sort of opportunities necessary for personal and community growth (Snow, 1991). Such organizing dreams take shape and gather force when people show their appreciation for another's gifts by listening carefully, affirming the dream by taking some action, waiting for the person's dream to clarify and deepen in response to affirmation, and challenging the person and other members of the circle to be faithful to the dream (Pearpoint, 1990). The dreams that focus circles are not arcane. Cathy's dream of a congenial housing cooperative doesn't require interpretation by a qualified analyst. It straightforwardly calls for her and members of her circle to do some hard work. Dreams are not blueprints. Kevin's dream of using his interest in computer graphics to make a living points a direction that will grow more clear as he tries things and discovers what works for him.

People with very little ability to communicate, people with limited experience, and people who have been oppressed into internal silence rely on others to begin to articulate a dream for them. Kevin's brother, Jason, challenges his family and friends with a vision of Kevin joining him at school. Kevin's enthusiasm and the energy this dream generates in the rest of the circle confirms Jason's dream for Kevin. Dreaming for another is, of course, dangerous: a vulnerable person could easily get trapped in what someone else thinks should be good for them. Dreaming for another must arise from a kind of love that includes recognition of the other person's separate identity. It is a dialogue of action in which circle members take a step and then carefully wait to see whether the person they are concerned for responds with a next step that confirms or redirects them.

Typical human service practice doesn't respond to people's dreams and support their capacities. It takes shape around professional accounts of people's deficiencies and policies designed to ration public funds. Kevin was excluded from opportunities to make friends and learn history by receiving the measure of service professionally judged to match his level of disability. Cathy couldn't set up her own home because service system policies deny her the number of hours of attendant services she requires. Kevin and Cathy were not excluded by accident or professional incompetence but by design and by professionals doing their jobs according to accepted practice. A circle that shrinks from confronting the injustice taken for granted in the lives of people with severe disabilities will quickly lose energy and direction. Action to follow Kevin and Cathy's dreams includes renegotiating the terms on which they get the assistance they need and redesigning policies that disadvantage them. Kevin's circle found a way around his school district's special education practice which allows him to be in school and to combine the extra help he needs in some areas with opportunities to enjoy the resources of regular teachers, students, and school activities. Cathy's circle searches for ways to provide her home through action outside disability services and the assistance she needs through changed policies. Changes for Kevin and Cathy set new precedents and help make policy changes that other people with severe disabilities can benefit from.

Circles of support are explicitly constructed with the specific intention of assisting the person at their center. Circle members gather regularly for meetings. Facilitators play an important role in helping a person organize a circle, guiding circle members in discovering the focus person's dream and making personal commitments to take action to help the focus person realize the dream, and supporting the continuous process of problem solving that structures the circle's work. Experienced facilitators have written guidelines and advice and developed facilitator training programs (Beeman, Ducharme, & Mount, 1989; Snow, 1989).

Invited people from Kevin's and Cathy's social networks commit themselves to form the support circles. Some people with limited contacts or ability to communicate rely on a close ally to extend the invitation, and many of the most powerful circles form around a strong one-to-one relationship (Snow, 1989). With the guidance of facilitators, Linda invited some of her friends and one of Kevin's contacts to join her family to clarify their collective sense of Kevin's future. Others make their own invitations. With the guidance of facilitators, Cathy invited her friends and her mother to join her in figuring out how to make her vision of a better life.

As the circle's work proceeds, its size and composition often changes. Members reach out through their own social networks to include others with needed talents. Some people leave the circle as the time for their contribution passes or their available energy decreases. When a circle forms around a child, facilitators often support the development of two somewhat interlocked circles: one circle of young people, usually focused on the school and social life of the child, and another circle focused on the parents (Snow & Forest, 1988).

Some circles develop a shifting focus: the person for whom the circle convened sometimes moves out of the center of the circle's concern and another circle member's needs take precedence for a time. Cathy particularly enjoys the fact that others can benefit from the focused energy of the circle she has organized.

Circles are contagious. Once some people have experienced their power they want to share it. One of the members of Cathy's circle formed a circle for herself, and several other people involved in circles formed by the project that supports Kevin and Cathy have learned to facilitate circles for other people.

Reflecting on her experience with support circles, Beth Mount (1991) identifies ten conditions associated with significant change. These conditions describe a support circle with a good chance of making a positive difference in the quality of a person's life.

- The focus person wants a change and agrees to work with a circle of support; support circles can't be forced on people
- All of the circle members, including the focus person, attend to the person's capacities and gifts and search for opportunities rather than dwelling on disabilities, deficiencies, and barriers.
- Circle members have chances to find out about new possibilities and new ways to organize the assistance the focus person needs
- The circle shares a clear vision of a different life for the focus person, and the vision vividly defines the kind of opportunities the focus person needs to share unique gifts and pursue individual interests
- At least one circle member has a strong commitment to act vigorously on the focus person's behalf.
- At least one circle member has a broad network of contacts in the focus person's local community and the skill and desire to help the focus person build ties to other people

- A skilled facilitator is available to the support circle
- Some support circle members are active in organizations and coalitions aimed at changing unjust or ineffective policies
- Some circle members develop influence with the people who make policy and administer human service programs that affect the quality of the focus person's life
- At least one human service program the focus person relies on has an explicit commitment to continuous improvement in its ability to support people's full participation in community life.

The stringency of these conditions is a measure of the distance between everyday life for people with severe disabilities and simple dreams like having friends, a job, and a home of one's own.

Circles of support offer people a structure for discovering and celebrating their membership in one another. By working together with someone who would be unable to realize an important dream without their support, circle members remember the human interdependencies which form the foundation of civic life.

How human services could help

Working outside the human service system, and frequently against opposition from service professionals, some citizens accomplish a great deal for the people they know and care for. Many parents have raised their severely disabled children as full participants in family and community life with little or no help from service programs (Schaefer, 1982). Citizen advocates have taken institutionalized children into their homes without professional sanction or support and helped families adapt or even build homes that allow them to better look after a severely disabled member (Bogdan, 1987). Circles of fellow students welcome, support, and protect severely disabled classmates in schools across North America (Perske, 1988).

However, it is unjust to expect that opportunities for people with severe disabilities should depend on heroic efforts to outwit segregating policies and work around misdirected professional practice. Human service programs can't substitute for freely given relationships; indeed, service programs destroy people's membership in community when they try to replace ordinary activities and relationships. But human services don't have to be the major obstacle to people's pursuit of their dreams.

Simple changes in common practice would create more room for relationships and memberships to form and grow. Service staff could reduce barriers...

...if they stopped acting as if they owned the people they serve and could arbitrarily terminate their contacts or disrupt their memberships

... if they modified schedules and tasks to accommodate people's relationships and memberships

... if they recognized and encouraged activities and contacts outside their programs

...if they looked for the flexibility to assist with some of the ideas and plans that emerge from new relationships and new memberships

These changes in attitude and practice would help some, but the work of community builders suggests important policy changes that add up to a system better able to assist people without destroying their sense of community membership.

Members of twelve different support circles in Connecticut developed thoughtful analyses of the human service policies that block opportunities for personal and family development, for good schooling, for employment, and for secure homes. They discussed the problems they identify and their proposed solutions in a series of policy forums that included political and administrative decision makers. Policy makers and administrators who want to be of genuine assistance, would follow these six directions:

- Increase the amount of personal assistance (attendant and family support) services available to people based on individual need by reallocating all funds that now support various forms of congregate long term care. Make personal assistance services more flexible by putting them under the direct control of the person who uses them, or, if the person is a child, under control of the child's family. Demedicalize personal assistance services.
- Insure that people with severe disabilities have an adequate cash income and adequate health insurance. Eliminate benefits traps that prevent people who want to work from doing so. Eliminate stigmatizing practices.
- Support individual or cooperative home ownership for adults with severe disabilities. Break programmatic links that tie people who need a particular type or amount of support to an agency owned building.
- Offer a wide variety of supports for individual employment in good jobs of people's choice.
- Insure that local schools fully include students with severe disabilities.

o Invest in safe and accessible transportation.

Within these policies, human service programs have a reasonable chance to develop the competencies necessary to assist people to pursue their own lives while maintaining community membership (Ferguson, Hibbard, Leinen, & Schaff, 1990).

Paradoxes of community building

The work of building communities in which people with severe disabilities are recognized members requires a talent for finding the truth in apparent contradictions. So far as community building has developed to date, paradox shapes the requirements of the work, and no one who insists on simple, unambiguous instructions can understand the work or do it well.

Each form of community building that we have described celebrates freely given contributions, but the people who invite and support these unpaid relationships are either paid to do so or earn their living in a way that lets them devote substantial time to this work. Overcoming the social forces that push and pull people with severe disabilities out of community requires hard, sustained work. It takes time to get to know people; it takes time to listen for people's interests; it takes time to seek out new opportunities; it takes time to make introductions; it takes time to give people the assistance they want with problem solving. Many of the people who freely offer the gift of hospitality and bring people into membership recognize an essential and usually continuing contribution from community building project staff (the citizen advocacy coordinator, the person paid to link people to associations, and the circle facilitator).

Community building staff frequently distance themselves from human service program staff, but they are themselves paid for their work with disabled people, most frequently out of grant funds earmarked for human services. Though it is clear that the work of community building can be destroyed when it is mixed up with the work of typical human service programs, its proper home and proper sources of funding are far from clear. Community building staff identify themselves with communities and their associations; but many community association leaders see and respect them as workers for disabled people. Community building staff speak eloquently of the benefits of inclusive community for all people, but many active citizens speak of themselves as finding satisfaction in helping the disabled.

Each form of community building celebrates the wisdom and

ability of ordinary citizens, but many ordinary citizens have so much difficulty recognizing their common membership with a severely disabled person that they need someone they recognize as an expert to ratify their competence. Many ordinary citizens feel uncomfortable in the world of disability services and need someone to tell them that their perceptions of people and situations and their ideas for action make sense even if they disagree with the psychologist; even if they don't understand the acronyms; even if they can't cite pertinent case law. Many people who have worked skillfully and faithfully to assist a person with a disability to overcome serious problems talk appreciatively of community building project staff as disability experts, however uncomfortable that may make the staff.

Practitioners of each form of community building celebrate actions that rescue people from the human service system and return them to the natural support of their community, but most of the severely disabled people now involved in community building efforts still rely substantially on human services, and many are almost totally controlled by service practices despite the committed involvement of ordinary citizens. Despite bureaucratic dreams of smooth coordination between service providers and advocates for individuals, the relationship between service providers and the people they serve remains fundamentally problematical. No system can be trusted to always know and pursue the best interests of each person. Every system balances support for individuals with the tasks of social control. Any system can slip into tyranny and abuse. So community building efforts won't succeed by ignoring basic conflicts of interest between severely disabled people and human service systems. But if it is hard for people with severe disabilities to live with flawed human service programs, it is harder for most to live without them. Citizen advocates, fellow association members, and circle members make a priceless contribution to people's well being; but very few of them have the social resources to sustain the people they care about completely outside the human service system. To act wisely, they need to recognize the inherent limits of service programs but then to identify and then to insist on the contributions that service programs can make to disabled people's well being. Those who ignore or belittle political action on an agenda like the one pursued by Connecticut's allied circle members, greatly reduce the possibility that severely disabled people will have the assistance they need to enjoy the opportunities that new memberships and new relationships open up to them.

Many people consider spontaneity the hallmark of personal relationships. Most everyone today would be uncomfortable with the idea of outsiders manufacturing and managing personal relationships, but community building efforts always involve carefully planned introductions which are usually followed with well organized efforts to resolve problems and pursue opportunities. It takes little more than a welcome to achieve a persons presence in an activity or an association. Becoming a full and valued participant takes conscious effort. Of course, work on a friendship or on inducting someone into full membership happens commonly, but this is usually the exclusive business of insiders. A third party (like a citizen advocacy coordinator, or a person whose job is helping associations to include people with disabilities, or a circle facilitator) seldom influences or orchestrates ordinary relationships and memberships. Some people reject any suggestion of systematic work to make and expand a valued place for someone who has been excluded because they feel that such efforts would be contrived or artificial. Yet without such work, many people with disabilities fall back into isolation.

These paradoxes define some of the most important issues for the future of explicit efforts to bring people from moral and social exclusion to membership. People concerned to build communities need to keep learning how to deal constructively with...

- Being paid supporters of voluntary efforts
- Being seen by many community members as somehow part of a system whose hold on people they, as community builders, are committed to undo
- Acting as disability experts whose message is that most disability specific expertise has little relevance
- Developing as many opportunities as possible outside the jurisdiction of a system of human service programs that virtually all people with severe disabilities will continue to depend upon
- Offering necessary structures to invite people to spontaneously develop positive relationships and satisfying associations.

Conclusion

Clear recognition of shared membership offers people a place in the web of friendships, exchange networks, and associations that support life. But many community members leave out people with severe disabilities when they count the people who belong with them in their neighborhoods, schools, work places, and cultural, political, and leisure activities. This unfortunate exclusion decreases the human diversity that can energize civic life, with obvious cost to people with severe disabilities and their families.

Given the opportunity to meet people with severe disabilities and share their lives and their dreams, many people overcome the pressures that deny their membership. Social innovators have created several ways to help people build positive relationships, increase the diversity of association membership, and take joint action to make positive changes.

Inclusion among the recognized members of a community cannot substitute for public investment in a variety of supports and opportunities for people with substantial, continuing need for assistance. Social support is not a substitute for well designed services; social support is the foundation for any effective service. Conflict involving excluded people will always be harder to resolve justly than conflict among members. Excluded people will always be more difficult to assist effectively than people whose common membership is recognized by all and celebrated by some.

Civic life depends on citizens' willingness to recognize and support one another's membership despite apparent differences. All people will live better lives when the knowledge that we are all members of each other shapes everyday life and collective decisions.

Unlikely Alliances

Nature assigns the Sun—
That—is Astronomy—
Nature cannot enact a Friend—
That—is Astrology.
-Emily Dickinson

Friendships can't be calculated by dispassionate observers, as the orbit of the sun can; but their meanings can be better understood by reflective participants, as other human mysteries can. Better understanding could make us better friends and wiser assistants to people for whom friendships are unlikely alliances because they are separated, and isolated, by prejudice against disability.

English language dictionaries mirror the ambiguity of friendship. In common usage, someone attached by feelings of affection is a friend, someone who acts as a patron or benefactor is a friend, and someone who is simply not hostile is a friend. This ambiguity helps to illuminate a dispute between a special education teacher and a mother who has successfully advocated for her son's inclusion in high school. The young man's teacher points with pride to his many friends. The teacher notes that almost everybody in school knows the young man's name and says 'hi" to him, and that some of the young women in his class have befriended him, as evidenced by their willingness to look after him on a class trip. The young man's mother says that, though he is well known in school, other students don't treat him as an equal or spontaneously involve him in their lives outside of school. She believes that people are friendly but that he has no real friends to count on. She wants the people who assist her son to think more deeply about friendship and to work in a more focused way to support others to become his friends. She says that it worries and angers her that the teacher can't understand her concern.

This disagreement over the meaning of friendship contains the questions that concern us in this chapter. What can people with

[2] Examples which are not otherwise referenced are drawn from notes and recordings we made during five, one day long focus group meetings on the topic of friendship and people with developmental disabilities. Three of these meetings involved parents and friends of people with developmental disabilities and were convened by the Association for Community Living in Colorado in January and June, 1992 and by the Wisconsin Coalition for Advocacy in March 1990. One meeting involved people who use services for adults with developmental disabilities. This meeting was convened by INFO, a self advocacy group active

developmental disabilities expect from their social relationships, particularly their relationships with people without disabilities? Is the meaning of 'friend' exhausted by lack of hostility or by benevolent patronage? Or are some deeper meanings possible, and, if they are, how can we understand them, call them forth, and support them? What challenges come with friendship?

We think that these are difficult questions for three reasons, each of which offers a guide to the kind of discussion appropriate to the topic. First, modern patterns of practice and belief segregate and isolate people with developmental disabilities as a matter of course. Outside of families and human service settings, sustained relationships of any sort involving people with developmental disabilities are unlikely alliances. Instead of being able to consider many and varied experiences which extend over generations, we can only draw on a few experiences, most of which are measured in much less time than a decade. So our discussion must be tentative, a way to find the next steps in a long journey newly begun.

Second, a great deal is at stake. People with developmental disabilities have suffered terrible consequences from being seen as less than human (Wolfensberger, 1975). However fuzzy or implicit the common understanding of friendship may be, most people would say that someone incapable of friendship is diminished in a basic quality of humanity. Aware of this, and moved by their own love, a growing number of parents of people with developmental disabilities hope powerfully for true, sustaining, and lasting friendships for their son's and daughter's pleasure and protection. Jeff and Cindy Strully spoke for many other parents when they said,

> *"It is friendship that will ultimately mean life or death for our daughter. It is her and our only hope for a desirable future and protection from victimization." (Strully & Strully, 1993)*

So our discussion must be careful never to compromise the human dignity of people with developmental disabilities and cautious not to betray hope with inflated stories of easy success or perfect relationships.

Third, friendship itself is problematic. Friendship has stimulated beautiful, wise, and whimsical thoughts about some of the highest and best human possibilities (see Welty & Sharp, 1991). And contemporary criticism exposes the elitist, individualistic, and patriarchal biases in the ways many thinkers have understood and shaped our society's written understanding of friendship (Heilbrun, 1988; McFague, 1987; Raymond, 1986). On some classical views, women could not be true friends, foreigners could not be true friends, people of low status could not be true friends. All of these groups lack the qualities of intellect and spirit and the social position assumed necessary for friendship (Benveniste, 1973; Easterling, 1989). On some modern

in the Northwest of England, in November 1990. This meeting is also reported in Flynn, 1991. The fourth meeting, which involved adult service providers and some of the people they support, was convened by the Ohio Society for Autistic Citizens in May, 1985. This meeting is also reported in Pealer & O'Brien, 1985.

views, friendship is aside and apart from the real, fundamentally competitive business of life. It matters mostly to women and children and only to men as a brief respite from the daily fight for a living (Lasch, 1978; Traustadottir, 1992). So our discussion needs to be critical of assumptions about friendship.

Four dimensions of friendship

Mary Hunt's (1991) consideration of friendship provides a good starting place because she calls attention to important aspects of friendship that are easily ignored in a culture given to individualism. Instead of focusing solely on its advantages to isolated individuals, Hunt sets friendship in the context of building up a more just community. Friendship, she believes, forms the goal of human community and the defining image of ethical relationships.

> *"Justice involves making friends, lots of friends, many kinds of friends... [who] empower one another to keep making change [in the structures and conditions that make friendship difficult or impossible]."* (p.21)

Hunt's reflections draw attention to four aspects of friendship; we have adapted them* in order to explore friendships that involve people with severe disabilities.

- **Attraction** points to the mystery that brings friends together and recognizes that friends feel some kind of unity which they can preserve, deepen, and express by being together. Friends may say they feel attracted by their similarities or by their differences. However it is explained, whether it is ever stated explicitly or not, attraction refers to the "something", noticed or discovered, that draws friends to one another and keeps relationships alive.
- **Embodiment** identifies the particular ways people physically enact friendship, which differ from person to person and from relationship to relationship. People may embody a friendship by watching movies together, making music together, running a business together, exchanging the news of daily life, writing letters back and forth, meeting once a year to fish, or raising children together.
- **Power** distinguishes the extent and the ways in which friends can make choices about their relationship for themselves as well as the accommodations friends make to the personal and structural constraints that affect their friendship.
- **Community** recognizes that friendships are situated within, and contribute to, the life of a civic and social body. The choices that friends make either build up or break down a community that can offer its diverse members justice and belonging.

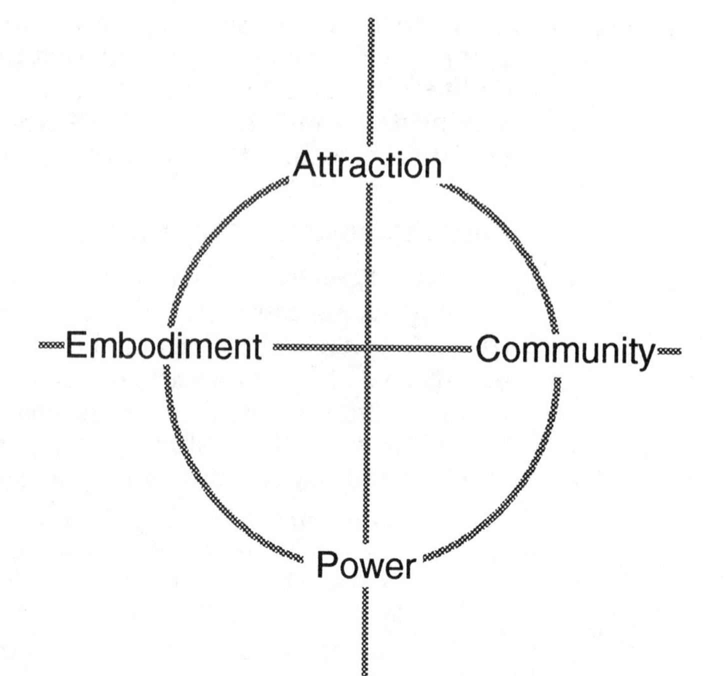

These four dimensions do not exhaustively define friendship; they simply identify important elements of its meaning. These dimensions of friendship matter particularly for people with developmental disabilities because the social construction of disability can make friendship particularly difficult for them. Community matters because people with developmental disabilities risk social devaluation -being seen as "not like the rest of us", even to the extent of being socially defined and treated as inhuman (Wolfensberger, 1991). Without the strength to resist, which is provided by a developing community, friendships cannot thrive. Power matters because disabled people typically have less of it than non-disabled people take for granted. Without action to deal with imposed inequality, friendships cannot thrive. Embodiment matters because people with developmental disabilities risk losing friends simply because they need assistance to undertake the activities that lead to and express friendship. Without effective assistance, friendships cannot thrive. Attraction matters because people with developmental disabilities have just as much capacity for friendship as any other people do. Because of the power of attraction, friendships can thrive.

* Hunt invites her readers to use her approach to stimulate conversation about friendships which will lead to new models (p. 100). We have accepted her invitation, maintained the overall structure of her model, and modified its terms to better fit our own reflections on friendships involving people with severe disabilities. Hunt identifies the four poles of the diagram below as "love", "embodiment", "power", and "spirituality" (p. 99) The words we have chosen retain the sense of Hunt's discussion.

The question of attraction

The question of attraction haunts many discussions about friendships for people with developmental disabilities. According to parents, there are at least three ways that others dismiss their concern for their children's friendships. Some people say that friendship is not a problem: people with developmental disabilities already have all the friends they need or want, especially among their "peers" -the other clients of congregate services. Some people say that friendship, as people without disabilities understand it, doesn't matter to people with developmental disabilities: people with developmental disabilities lack the capacity to understand it. Some people say that friendships, particularly friendships including people without disabilities, are an unrealistic dream: people with and without disabilities have too little in common to make friends. These three dismissals have a similar element. Each assumes that people with and without disabilities will not discover and pursue mutual attractions because of the way people with disabilities are.

Are people with developmental disabilities able to attract people without disabilities?

Summarizing his discussion of human development, Robert Kegan observed,

> *Who comes into a person's life may be the single greatest factor of influence to what that life becomes. Who comes into a person's life is in part a matter of luck, in part a matter of one's power to recruit others, but in large part a matter of other people's ability to be recruited. People have as varying capacities to be recruited as they do to recruit others.* (Kegan, 1982, p. 19)

Does disability necessarily lead to low capacity to recruit and be recruited? Can people with developmental disabilities recruit people without disabilities into their lives? Are people without disabilities recruitable by people with disabilities?

The experience of many families clearly answers, yes! People with developmental disabilities can powerfully recruit others into their lives and activate good relationships through which people work for social justice. Based on his study of six families, three of whom adopted their children with disabilities, Biklen (1992) concludes that the kinds of positive relationships that these families work to achieve within themselves should guide public policy and educational practice. Schools should support all children, unconditionally, to be full participants in every day life, as these six families strive to do. Professionals should recognize and assist people's natural desire to be fully involved in life, as these six families strive to do. Other people should make the chance to discover and enjoy people's individual gifts, as these six families strive to do. These families fully include and work to expand opportunities for their disabled member, not from a sense of pity or duty, but because their appreciation of his or her identity flows into a clear sense of what is right.

Dorothy Atkinson (1986) studied the relationship networks of the 28 women and 27 men discharged between 1971 and 1981 from the institutions serving one English county. She found that all but seven people had involved at least one neighbor in social and helpful relationships. Almost three-fourths of the people had non-disabled acquaintances they see regularly, and about half the people had at least one supportive friend without a disability. She notes that these people without disabilities make a real and sustained contribution to the lives of people with developmental disabilities, offering information, advice, assistance, support, conversation, and company.

One reason that these positive images of relationship have not yet been influential in shaping policy and practice is that attention has focused elsewhere. During the past twenty-five years of service reform, concern for the rights of people with developmental disabilities overshadowed attention to their relationships.

As Steven Taylor and Robert Bogdan point out, many workers took up the sociology of deviance as an effective tool to explain, guide, and justify their reforms. This understanding of the negative effects of stigmatizing labels and practices fueled the fight for equal rights for people with developmental disabilities and led to much positive change, but

> *...it has too often been interpreted in terms of the inevitability of rejection of people with obvious differences... labeling and exclusion of people with disabilities have become so taken-for-granted that instances of acceptance have been glossed over or ignored. (Taylor & Bogdan, 1989, p. 25)*

To complement the understanding offered by a sociology of deviance, Bogdan and Taylor have begun to outline a sociology of acceptance, based on the recognition that some people with and without disabilities have formed long standing, close, and affectionate relationships which neither deny disability nor stigmatize a person on the basis of disability. In such relationships, people without disabilities see, enjoy, celebrate, and protect the positive qualities, the abilities, and the individuality of people whose disabilities loom very large to most people outside the relationship (see Bogdan & Taylor, 1987; Bogdan & Taylor, 1990 & Taylor & Bogdan, 1989).

Why do so many people with developmental disabilities lack friends? If people with disabilities can recruit others into their lives, and if accepting relationships are possible, a reasonable person might mistakenly think that friendships will take care of themselves. Maybe people will have few friends among people without disabilities, but certainly they will have many good friends among people with developmental disabilities.

A survey of US residential programs asked knowledgeable staff about contacts between older clients of residential services and their friends (Anderson, Lakin, Hill, & Chen, 1992). The survey broadly defined a friend as a person other than a family member with whom the resident looks forward to spending time, either at the facility or somewhere else. Under this definition a friend might be another resident (and about 30% of the time, staff identified another resident as a person's closest friend) or it might be a non-disabled person (and about 14% of the time, staff identified a non-disabled person as the resident's friend) or it might be another disabled person. The survey estimates that about half of people with mental retardation over 63 years of age either have no friends at all or never see their friends. Only 25% of those people staff identified as having friends see a friend once a month or more. Compounding this group's isolation, about half have no contact at all with their families.

Unfortunately, this level of isolation does not appear to result just from the age of the people involved. In a larger survey, representative of the whole US population in residential programs for people with mental retardation, staff in close contact told interviewers that about 42% of people in community programs and about 63% of people in institutions had no friends, even among other residents or staff (Hill, Rotegard, & Bruininks, 1984). This study defined a friend as anyone the resident liked and did things with on the resident's own time.

These findings call for action, and the researchers who report them have sensible recommendations to offer: prefer smaller residential settings over larger settings because the surveys show that smaller settings offer people more social contacts; increase people's involvement with neighbors (about two-thirds of whom were described by staff informants in the study of older residents as either "warm and accepting" or "friendly"); increase people's use of ordinary community places such as shops, churches, libraries, and parks; increase attention to peoples leisure time opportunities; and concentrate staff attention on building up people's social contacts. But these finding also deserve thoughtful, even meditative, consideration: why do so many people have no friends?

Do people have friendships that are invisible to outsiders?

Perhaps these findings say more about the difference between life as people with developmental disabilities live it and the lives that staff or other outsiders can see. Maybe there are many more friendships among people with developmental disabilities than are apparent to observers. Anne McDonald, who survived fifteen years in an institution for "profoundly mentally retarded children", describes friendships among inmates that were invisible not just to ordinary staff, but to her teacher, ally, and friend Rosemary Crossley as well. Some people that staff assumed incapable of communication were, it turns out, not babbling and shrieking but conversing. Once Anne could communicate with staff, however, she kept these relationships secret for two reasons: she feared that even Rosemary, her closest ally, would not believe that her friendships were real; and, she thought that if staff suspected that these friendships existed, staff would break them up in order to retain control of the ward (Crossley & McDonald, 1984).

Poet Robert Williams (1989) expresses this disjunction of perception in "Dick and Jane," Dick and Jane are institutionalized lovers who have "shared the same mat since they were children" and who find pleasure in one another's touch:

> *...they move an inch or two closer to each other*
> *hoping that the staff doesn't pick up on the subtleties*
> *of the moment;*
> *they don't of course. (p. 13)*

Knowledge of the possibility of invisible friendships instills caution on two counts: people with authority to move people with developmental disabilities around will consider people's relationships when they make decisions about such movements (Berkson & Romer. 1981); and outsiders will be careful to remember the limitations of their point of view, keep open the possibility that much more is happening than they know, and inquire actively for different perspectives, especially the perspectives of the involved people with disabilities. However, the possibility of invisible friendships does not imply that all people in congregate residences and day programs have friends, and it does not engage the question of friendships between people with developmental disabilities and people without disabilities.

Indeed, if staff cannot even recognize some friendships among people with developmental disabilities, there could be such a gulf between the experiences of people with and without disabilities that friendship between them is unattainable. There is, however, a simpler explanation for this lack of staff awareness. The norms and beliefs that organize most service settings into distinct, unequal sub-cultures of keepers and inmates explain staff's blindness better than the argument that people with developmental disabilities are a kind of distinct sub-species does (Barnes, 1990; Glouberman, 1990). Concern for friendship means hard work to minimize the status and power differences between people with disabilities and the people who assist them. Only then will concerned people be able to better appreciate individual differences and more accurately describe the social worlds of people with disabilities.

Do friendships matter to people with developmental disabilities?

Of course, even within the closed environments of congregate services, staff do see friendships. Staff surveyed in the studies summarized above said that about half the people do have friendships: mostly with other residents. But they may not think they are seeing friendships like their own. Any possibility of friendship, even friendships among people with developmental disabilities themselves, has been in question within the lifetime of many adults now alive. A special education teacher in a segregated community program provided this explanation of why her moderately mentally retarded students had few social contacts:

> *They don't have friends because they don't have much in the way of a self concept. So they don't value the esteem of others. (Evans, 1983, p. 122).*

MacAndrew and Edgerton (1966) summarized a thorough and sensitive description of a ten year relationship with these words:

> *We have outlined what we take to be the principal characteristics of a highly improbable, strikingly pervasive and intense friendship between two severely retarded young men. Hopefully, we have provided sufficient detail to convince the reader that this long enduring and highly elaborated relationship is indeed a friendship of a highly human order. The existence of such a relationship between two persons of such enfeebled intellect must be counted as compelling testimony to the essentially human character of even the most retarded among us. (p. 620, emphasis in original)*

Even when they are recognized, friendships among people with developmental disabilities may be trivialized. Patrick Worth (1990), a leader in the People First movement, shared his experience in a group home and a sheltered workshop:

> *Staff put down our friendships when they didn't try and break them up. They acted like our friends were less than their friends. It's like they were saying, "Isn't it nice that you have your little friends to play with." When a friend got sick and you asked to go to the hospital and see him, they acted like you were being foolish. When a friend got in trouble and had to go to a discipline meeting, they acted like you were from Mars when you said you wanted to go to the meeting with him. "It's none of your business," they said. "We have to protect confidentiality," they said. Like we didn't talk to our friends about the trouble they were in. Like we didn't owe our friends any help. And sometimes a friend got moved away without even having a chance for us to say good bye.*

Seeing friendship through the lens of quantitative research can also have the effect of trivializing friendships. Defining a friend as a person "other than family or staff with whom the resident looks forward to spending time" (Anderson, Lakin, Hill, & Chen, 1992, p. 493) powerfully documents people's isolation -since only about 1 in five people have weekly contact with such friends- but it doesn't begin to touch common understandings of friendship. Lining up a corps of volunteers to provide individual recreation in facilities might give residents an activity to look forward to, but it would only provide them with friends in the most diluted sense of the term.

In a study based on coding the behavior of 208 people living in 18 group homes, based on observations at 15 minute intervals over a two day period, Landesman-Dwyer, Berkson, & Romer (1979) operationally defined friendship as "those pairs [of residents] who spent more than 10% of the observed time periods together" (p. 576). By this method, they discovered 16 "peer friendships." They conclude that

> *...group home characteristics are better predictors of social behavior... than are individual variables.... For instance... in homes where the average intelligence is higher, residents are likely to spend more time in peer relationships. (578)*

This way of understanding friendship sets people who live in group homes apart both by the peculiar, diminished image of friendship it projects and prescribes for them and by its loud silence about the possibility of friendships between residents and people without disabilities: its definition even rules out residential staff as potential friends. The implications of the study are also of questionable utility. Manipulating the variables of group home design to increase the number of pairs of people who spend 10% of their time together might not increase the number of people with developmental disabilities who have others to share with and count on.

As others listen better to people with developmental disabilities, the gap between the worlds of people with and without disabilities diminishes, and a common sense of friendship emerges. Consider the powerful ordinariness of this woman's description of friendship, taken from an anthology of writings and art work by British people with developmental disabilities.

> *As I've got older, I've got few friends and lots of acquaintances. A friend is one who knows all about you and loves you just the same; A friend to me is someone really special. Even if we don't see each other for years we can pick up where we've left off. I've got one friend I've known for 34 years.* (Atkinson & Williams, 1990, p. 78)

Can relationships between people with and without disabilities be friendships?

People with developmental disabilities share activities with people without disabilities, and people without disabilities establish accepting relationships with people with developmental disabilities, but some wonder about considering these relationships friendships. Assigned to identify the practical implications of Robert Perske's *Circles of friends* (1988), some of the participants in a staff training course expressed skepticism about whether the relationships Perske described were really friendships. They asked: What do the people involved really have in common? Can these be equal relationships? What do the people with developmental disabilities contribute? Do people with limited language understand the relationship?

These questions reflect some sensible criteria for defining friendship: common interests, equality, mutuality, and understanding. In her careful study of four friendships involving people with and without disabilities, Zana Lutfiyya (1989; 1990) makes two important points about these criteria. First, the meaning of any friendship is created by the ways in which its participants enact and talk about it. Commonalty, equality, mutuality, and comprehension are best understood from the perspective of the friends themselves, rather than according to the measurements of a detached observer. Second, according to the people in them, these criteria are satisfied in the relationships she studied.

Despite the differences in opportunities and experiences, at least some people with disabilities have successfully formed friendships with non disabled people. Through studying established friendships, we learn that both parties possess a respect for the other. The friends also experienced a mutuality in their interactions that may not be apparent to the outside observer. These feelings stem from a sense of identification between the two individuals. They come to see the "sameness" or commonalities between themselves and these serve as the basis of the relationship... (Lutfiyya, 1990, p. 74.)

Jeff and Cindy Strully have grappled with the meaning of friendship for people with limited verbal communication as they have worked hard to support friendships for their daughter Shawntell. They report (Strully & Strully, 1985; 1989; 1992) on her changing relationships from their perspective and from the perspective of the young women who are Shawntell's friends. Biklen (1992) provided a helpful metaphor for the construction of meaning in these relationships. He suggested that, when someone's verbal communication is very limited, concerned others can read the person's behavior and expressions, giving voice to them as if they were a text. Like the members of the families Biklen studied, Shawntell's friends read their shared activities and their reactions to one another as signifying friendship. Through time, Shawntell's responses to going out for dinner with them, taking holiday trips with them, going to concerts, sports events and parties with them, listening to music with them, hanging out at school and around the house with them, and driving around town with them, all mean that they are friends. They speak of sharing confidences with Shawntell. They can identify her preferences and interests, overlapping but distinct from their own. They speak of trusting her and of learning from her. They talk about keeping up with one another as their paths in life diverge. They identify themselves to others as friends.

It is worth considering the messages in these questions about whether people with and without developmental disabilities can enjoy common interests, equality, mutuality, and understanding. The questions themselves suggest a sense of disability and of friendship narrowed and flattened by limited experience. Shawntell and Joyce are two young women of similar age and socio-economic status who attended the same high school and choose to spend considerable time together. To wonder what they have in common, one would need to place very great weight indeed on the effect of developmental disability on a person's interests or on the way a person is perceived. To wonder about their equality, one would need to assume that disability necessarily means inferiority. To wonder about what they exchange, or whether Shawntell comprehends the friendship, one would have to estimate that expressed verbal intelligence plays the defining role in friendship.

Notice the potential for self-fulfilling prophecy. Those who decide that disability overshadows anything people might discover in common, that disability equals inferiority, and that friendships are conducted primarily in spoken sentences will neither seek nor support relationships between people with and without disabilities. Those who decide to share some of their life with someone apparently different, as Shawntell's friends have done, can create a relationship that seems significant but unremarkable to them. When outsiders ask about the "special" nature of their friendship, they will say, as Shawntell's friends do, that they are "just friends; no big deal."

Estimating a low potential for friendship because of apparent differences between people reflects a narrow and flat appreciation of friendship and how it grows. As the dominant modern way of understanding relationships, individualism assumes that each party acts as a separated, closed entity exchanging units of advantage or enjoyment with the other. From this point of view, as long as the score balances out, the two parties can be said to have a friendship; if either scorekeeper predicts a low rate of return, no friendship can happen.

An understanding of friendship as dialogue offers a much richer medium for its growth. On this view, people become more deeply themselves, as individuals, only in relationship to a variety of different others. People learn who they are by discovering new modes of expressing themselves along with others. Relationship with somebody different can induct a person into new possibilities for self-expression (Booth, 1988, Chapter 8; Taylor, 1991). Socrates communicates this in the form as well as the content of the Lysis (Plato, 1979). He demonstrates a way to make a friend through a discussion about friendship in which he enlarges both his understanding of himself and his circle of friends. Creating a friendship between a person with and a person without a developmental disability opens new kinds of self-expression and new definitions of self for both people. Balance in relationships understood as dialogue is more like the balance between dancers than the balance on a bank statement.

Clearly, friendship should not be ignored or trivialized because of developmental disability and friendship need not be limited by disability. Among many others, Anne McDonald and her friends (Crossley & McDonald, 1984) show that people with disabilities can make friends even in the most restrictive settings, that people with and without disabilities can make friends, even in those same restricted circumstances, and that these friendships can last and grow even stronger as the people involved come out of segregation. Along with Shawntell Strully and her friends, they demonstrate that these diverse relationships can thrive despite obvious differences in personal history, embodied experiences, abilities, and status. However, even when concerned people are inspired by its possibilities, friendships between people with and without developmental disabilities remain uncommon. Why?

The challenges of embodiment

Friends enact their relationship; they do their friendship in ways distinctive of the interests they share. As one man with a developmental disability put it,

> *"I have two fishing friends and we fish. I have four football friends and we watch games and bet. I have three talking friends and we have a drink and talk -sometimes we go out and sometimes we come over to somebody's house. One of my friends is all three: fishing, and football, and talking. I also have a gardening friend and we ask about our gardens and talk about how to grow things and give each other cuttings. I also have a friend that was my teacher a long time ago and I go visit her and remember about bygone days."*

Each embodiment of this man's friendships takes time and other resources specific to the activity. He needs to get to where the fish are and have the tackle to catch them; he needs the plot to garden in and the seeds to plant; he needs the money to buy a round of drinks when his turn comes.

The social consequences of disability challenge the embodiment of relationships. Some challenges arise in the external world and some are part of people's personal experiences.

Some external challenges

Difficulty in getting places easily and safely challenges friendships. Most people with developmental disabilities are pedestrians in a society that expects automobiles. Fewer and fewer neighborhoods offer a rich and accessible social life within walking or rolling distance, and many residential facilities are physically isolated. Convenient, affordable public transportation remains uncommon. Always asking for rides, or being one of a group of passengers in the facility's van, are typical experiences.

Most people with developmental disabilities are poor, and many activities cost money. One woman noted that she watches television most nights "because the TV's paid for."

Many places people want to go together, including many people's homes, are either physically inaccessible or very inconvenient to use.

People's time may not be their own. For people who are full time clients of developmental disability services, getting together with friends raises issues of control. Requirements for active treatment and restrictions on movement and outside contact, driven by service provider concern for regulatory compliance and liability, often leave people literally without free time.

Many people with developmental disabilities who live with their families report that their parents don't allow them to go out, or prefer that they not go out, except with the family or to supervised disability activities.

Staff concern for the isolation of people with developmental disabilities can result in direct, practical assistance in trying new experiences, making acquaintances, and making friends (see Firth & Rapley, 1990; Richardson & Ritchie, 1989). This concern takes a different turn if friendship becomes the intended outcome of a rehabilitation process. Staff can decide that the road to friendship leads through correct performance on a professionally prescribed curriculum of social skills. A brochure describing one such program identifies 21 skills "selected to address the most common behavior problems exhibited by people with developmental disabilities", including "...having a calm body and voice, interrupting the right way, [and] accepting no as an answer...." These approaches set up artificial pre-requisites to friendship, based on an abstract analysis of assumed social deficiencies in people with developmental disabilities. This extension of staff control leaves many people waiting in vain for performance in role plays to result in real friends.

Lack of adequate help with mobility and communication inhibits the enactment of people's friendships. For example, facilitated communication is a method for assisting written communication by some people with autism and other physical problems in producing speech (Biklen, 1990). Facilitated communication has given some people whom others believed were asocial and incompetent the opportunity to communicate their interests and desires. With the physical assistance of a facilitator, Kim types,

> *my friends and me*
> *at rye high school i have friends*
> *they like me for me*
> *it feels like some magic*
> *how come i can't be like all the girls.*
> *(Bevilacqua, 1992, p. 6)*

People with developmental disabilities are often socially disembodied. Friendships emerge among a variety of social relationships, including being part of a family, having a life partner, being a neighbor, being part of a workplace, and being a member of community associations (Ordinary Life Group, 1988). The more of these ties and connections a person misses, the fewer opportunities and supports the person has to meet and make friends.

Current policies and program designs seldom offer people with developmental disabilities flexible personal assistance to pursue activities with acquaintances and friends. Even staff from an exemplary supported living program reported, with remorse, that they are unable to consistently find time to help people become better connected to their community.

Pervasive unfamiliarity with people with developmental disabilities can make many people without disabilities uneasy about initial contacts. Uncertainty about whether one will understand a person, and when and how to offer help can keep people at a distance (Williams, P., 1977). Men are often uncomfortable offering help, especially help with eating or using the toilet. This gendered reluctance can restrict people's friendships to women (Traustadottir, 1992). People without disabilities, perhaps especially young men, may fear that their own status will suffer by close association with people with developmental disabilities.

Some thoughtful people with physical disabilities believe that friendships among people with different disabilities are easier, and in some political and cultural ways more desirable, than efforts to make friends with people without disabilities. They point to the continuing experience of being seen and treated by non-disabled people as somehow unfamiliar, unwelcome, and inferior as a strong reason for putting priority on friendships with other people with disabilities. As Judith Heumann writes,

> *Disabled people's desire to be accepted by non-disabled people has been a cause of internal discrimination. I believe that we must first accept ourselves and then if non-disabled people don't accept us, so be it." (1993 p. 240).*

She goes on to provide welcome criticism of the assumption that

> *...the most important thing for us would be to be with non-disabled people.... I am concerned about the continued discussion of the percentages of disabled people and the appropriate statistical balance of disabled and non-disabled people as opposed to a balance based on interests, social aspirations, and professional aspirations." (p. 245)*

To the extent that people with and without disabilities come to feel that friendships between them are somehow incorrect, they will narrow their search for friends instead of widening it.

Accepting relationships are possible, but widespread, unthinking prejudice against people with developmental disabilities remains a fact of life. Some people act as though people with developmental disabilities were repulsive or dangerous and scorn or shun them. Some people act as though people with developmental disabilities were passive, pitiable creatures and intrusively try to be their helpers or saviors. Some people act as though people with developmental disabilities had no sense or will of their own and look for a trained staff person or a parent figure to talk to instead of relating directly to the person. As one man with a developmental disability put it:

> *I think the hardest part is you gotta defend yourself.... You gotta fight a, a reputation. People decide they know everything they need to know about me before they meet me even. They never get close enough to see if there is something inside they might like after all.* (Melberg-Schwier, 1990, p. 161-162)

Some personal challenges

Making and keeping friends takes energy and willingness to extend oneself. People with developmental disabilities participating in a conference on friendship identified three negative, self-reinforcing patterns of personal effects of the external challenges to friendship described above. In the first pattern, a person lacks experience with other people, or has had bad experiences with reaching out to others, and so lacks confidence. Lack of confidence keeps the person in, engaged in passive pursuits like watching television. This keeps the person from gaining experience and, over time, further decreases confidence. This pattern gets worse when the person eats and drinks too much to deal with loneliness, and so decreases the amount of energy available for reaching out. Conference participants felt that repeated invitations and encouragement's from others would help a person break out of this pattern.

In the second pattern, a person feels hurt inside because the person has been hurt, rejected, or abandoned by someone important. For protection the person makes a shell to keep others away. It may be a prickly shell, so that if someone tries to come close the person will hurt them to try to make them go away. It may be a hard shell, so that someone who tries to come close will feel like the person doesn't care about them. A woman who responded strongly to the image of a shell said,

> *I know my parents love me and only did what they thought was best. But they put me in the institution when I was only a very little girl. For a long, long time I cried and cried because*

I missed them so much. Then I stopped crying. I think about this, but I still have my prickly shell. Knowing about it doesn't make it go away.

This pattern gets worse when people get psychoactive drugs to control behavior which is unacceptable because staff and physicians understand its functions poorly, because, as one man said,

The right pills might help, I guess, But if you get the wrong pills, they take all the interest out of you."

Conference participants felt that others would need to be ready to take time and forgive a person caught up in this pattern for trying to hurt them, and that they would need to be unafraid and keep trying to make friends with the person anyway. They also thought it was important to tell the person when the person was hurting them and to realize that the person may not want to be too close.

Maureen Oswin (1992) echoes this pattern when she describes the all too common practice of denying people with developmental disabilities the opportunity and support to grieve important losses. She explains this deprivation by identifying a mistaken notion that people with developmental disabilities lack the resources to comprehend, cope with, and grow through their losses. She associates failure to support people in bereavement with chronic depression, physical complaints, and "unexplained" anger.

In the third pattern, a person feels safe and comfortable because of the familiarity of the relationships the person already has and the person fears the uncertainty of change. As one man said,

My mother and dad and me are very close. Sometimes I'd like to go out more on my own, but they really need me at home for company. My home could be a safe base to go out from, but it's a nice safe place to stay in. And I'm not sure other people would be as nice." Conference participants felt that a person caught in this pattern should not be forgotten, but invited to share activities repeatedly, so that they know they have a choice.

This third pattern seems to be related to the decisions described by Robert Edgerton (1988, 1991) as he summed up his learning from more than 20 years of research with people developmentally disabilities who live in the community:

Each person... realizes that it is sometimes, even often, necessary to seek help from others, and although these people may provide badly needed assistance, with that assistance may come unwanted advice, restrictions, or interference. When this happens, the person with mental retardation must decide, like the rest of us must, whether we need someone's help badly enough to surrender some of our autonomy. What is central in the lives of these older people is the search for well being, and that search involves an ever shifting calculus that attempts to balance freedom of choice against the need for the help of others. (1991, p. 273)

Aware of these personal barriers to enacting friendship, some people advocate individually focused counseling or training as the way to friendships. Aware of the negative effects of socially devaluing attitudes, others call for large scale public education as a pre-requisite to integration. Neither of these approaches seems preferable to vigorous effort alongside people with developmental disabilities to tear down those external barriers that are within reach. Many challenges to making friends result, directly or indirectly, from the negative effects of common practices by the staff and programs that people with developmental disabilities rely on for assistance. Work to reverse these practices makes the best investment in improving the chances for good relationships.

Some people with disabilities, and some people without disabilities, want and could benefit from counseling to sort out personal difficulties in making and keeping relationships. However, greater autonomy, more money, better transportation, flexible and available personal assistance, and more respect from those who provide assistance seem prerequisite to the effectiveness of counseling or skill training.

Widely held prejudices will only change slowly, with increasing personal contact between people with and without disabilities, and it is unlikely that prejudice will ever be eradicated. It makes more sense to offer people practical help to realize that prejudice co-exists with the potential for acceptance than it does to wait for implementation of grand plans to educate the public. People who act on this realization will encourage people with developmental disabilities to find and build up the many accepting relationships that are already potentially available.

Issues of power

Power enters into friendships between people with and without developmental disabilities in two connected ways. First, friends have to deal with constraints imposed on their relationship by outsiders who control the circumstances of the person with a developmental disability. Second, friends have to negotiate power differences between themselves. Failure to respond effectively to either of these issues of power threatens the strength and endurance of the friendship.

Pushing back constraints

Many people with developmental disabilities live and spend the day in situations where others have power over them. Even when staff in direct contact treat people with respect, impersonal others - service administrators and policy makers- retain power over them. This imbalance of power, and the responses friends make to it, shapes their friendships.

Most residential settings manage friends' access to one another. This control is sometimes explicit, as when friends have to have their contacts approved by an interdisciplinary team, or when friends without disabilities are required to undergo some form of training as a condition of spending time with their friend, or when staff members are forbidden to invite a friend home for a meal because it would violate wage and hour regulations. Other times, control of access is less direct: people have no privacy; visits with friends are interrupted by program routines; messages get lost; activities that require some cooperation from program staff break down because someone didn't pass along the right permission slip or the van has been re-routed.

One of the greatest powers service settings exercise is the power of definition. Staff define who the person with a developmental disability is and what is good for him or her. They assert the authority to say how it really is for a client. Often this process of definition reflects a preoccupation with finding fault in the person. A staff member describes a person with a developmental disability to the person's friend as manipulative, and cautions the friend against being "sucked into" or "feeding" the person's dependency. A staff member nods knowingly when a friend makes a positive comment about a person with a developmental disability and says sagely, "I thought that too, when I first met her." A staff member discounts ideas about a positive future as "unrealistic" or "inappropriate for someone who functions at that level." A staff member passes along comments about syndromes and symptoms.

Even when service workers enthusiastically endorse a plan for change, the systems they work in often respond ineptly and painfully slowly. Months can pass between a victory in a planning meeting and the first hint of real change.

Friends have to decide how to respond to these expressions of power over the person with a disability. The person's continuing need for assistance makes this a complex problem. Some people with developmental disabilities fear offending the people they rely on. Some people without disabilities doubt their own perceptions when they run counter to professional judgments.

Friends may decide to push back. Nicola is a 21 year old woman who attends a day program for people with developmental disabilities. A group of six of her friends, with whom she regularly shares a variety of social activities, reviewed her individual program plan together and wrote a letter to her IPP team which begins:

> *It's Tuesday night and we're all together with Nic. In the pub. We have just read your report... with disbelief, we're not so sure that we are discussing the same person...*
>
> *We don't see Nic in the same light as you do, and we feel you need to see the Nic that we know, because otherwise we don't think Nic's best interests will be served...*

They go on to make several concrete suggestions for assistance that they believe would be more relevant and better focus her strengths. The service system made no effective response to their comments.

The response from a threatened system can be much less benign. Working as a staff trainer in an institution, Rosemary Crossley discovered that several inmates were able to communicate, given assistance by someone who cares about what they have to say. Rosemary's discovery created close, increasingly personal relationships between her and several of the young people involved, including Anne McDonald, who ultimately came to live with Rosemary and her partner (Crossley & McDonald, 1984). Her personal engagement led her to challenge the constraints of the institution in a number of ways, including, spending her free time with Anne and other residents, taking Anne home for weekends and holidays, creating techniques and materials to support further communication, feeding Anne and other residents, working the bureaucratic system for a variety of resources, and, ultimately, helping Anne get a lawyer to free her from the institution. From very early in their relationship, these activities threatened the institutional system which reacted by invoking medical authority to publicly discredit Rosemary and her assertion that Anne and several other young people were able to think and communicate, demoting her, forbidding her to visit outside work hours, transferring her, and separating the group of young people involved. Elks (1990) helpfully analyzes the situation by contrasting the approach of Rosemary, a personally involved ally, with the institution professional approach like this:

Dimension of Difference	Personally Involved Ally	Institution Professionals
Overriding concern	Quality of life	Efficiency of operation
Involvement	Personal, daily, all hours, hands on, informal	Professional consultation, formal, day appointments only
Assessment issues & standards of proof	Open to all, informal, common sense, anecdotal, subjective	Professional only, formal, scientific, controlled, objective
Sources of support & power	Friends, media, courts, independent professionals	Bureaucratic & professional authority, legislation
Preferred way to make change	Personal & direct response to needs	"Normal [official] channels"
Gender	Female	Male
Status	Low	High
Conceptualization of controversy	Civil rights versus institutional denial & obstruction	Professional judgments versus irrational & emotional lay opinion

Negotiating differences in power

Power issues arise within any relationship. Questions between friends about how to make decisions, how to share resources and tasks, and how to deal with conflicts, which are common to all relationships are sharper in a friendship between a person with and a person without a developmental disability. This is because there is typically a power difference between the friends: one friend can come and go relatively freely and the other friend's time and movement may be under staff control; one friend may have more disposable income than the other; one friend may have transportation while the other does not; one friend may be seen by others as capable while the other is not; one friend may feel confident about changing jobs or living places while the other is unable to.

The person with less power usually sees and feels this difference more clearly than the more powerful person does. People without disabilities take for granted many small everyday powers which are privileges in the world of the person with a disability.

When a person with a developmental disability needs regular physical or cognitive assistance from a friend, the friendship can be strained. One woman with a developmental disability said,

> *I liked my friend a lot, but I stopped calling her because she can't come to the group home because its so noisy and so I was always having to ask her for rides.*

This kind of resource sharing is easier to resolve, once people bring it up, than the issues that arise when a person with a developmental disability has limited experience of relationships or a limited repertoire of expression and treats friend as if they were staff people, or parents, or servants.

Sometimes the friend with a developmental disability has very, very few ties and connections to anyone other than the friend without a disability. This can leave the person who has a wider social network feeling like the person with a developmental disability wants more from the relationship than the person without a disability can give. This problem is exaggerated when the friends embody their relationship in a narrow range of activities. As one man with a developmental disability put it,

> *We love the same football team. So some parts of the year we see each other all the time. Other parts of the year, I miss him a lot.*

People with disabilities may strongly and repeatedly test their friends because their personal history makes trust crucial to them. Anne McDonald risked her freedom, and jeopardized Rosemary Crossley's credibility, by refusing to cooperate with tests that would prove her ability to communicate to outsiders. As she explained in a conversation with Rosemary after refusing to respond compliantly to an investigating magistrate's questions,

> *Stubbornness is both my salvation and my besetting sin.... If surviving depended on any characteristic it was stubbornness: not letting the bastards grind you down.* (Crossley & McDonald, 1984, p. 239).

Someone whose life experiences have not included living in an institution, or living with continual discrimination, may have difficulty comprehending these tests for what they are, opportunities to deepen and strengthen the friendship.

Finally, friends can fail in their efforts to deal with injustice or achieve the cooperation necessary from others to move toward a better future. Failure can bring hurt, uncertainty, and even resentment. Friends without a disability may wonder if they have done enough. Friends with a disability may even feel that somehow they have let their friends down.

Signals of real differences in power between friends can make dealing with these hurts and conflicts harder. Anthropologist Mary Catherine Bateson (1988) observed American's discomfort with relationships that do not seem to be symmetrical,

> *...the ethical impulse in American culture is toward symmetry.... Nothing in our tradition gives interdependency a value*

comparable to symmetry. It is difference that makes interdependency possible, but we have difficulty valuing it because of the speed at which we turn it into inequality. This means that all of the relationships in which two people complement each other -complete each other, as their differences move them toward a shared wholeness- man and woman, artist and physician, builder and dreamer- are suspected of unfairness unless they can be reshaped into symmetrical collegiality. But symmetrical relationships and exchanges alone are limiting... (pp. 104-105)

Real differences in power create the possibility that people with and without disabilities can transcend ordinary social patterns and develop a friendship which allows interdependence.

Friendship as a way to human development

To sustain friendship through struggles with external constraints and internal contradictions, friends need a deeper way to understand friendship than many contemporary accounts offer. Friendship, especially friendship across a structural imbalance in power, requires endurance, discipline and courage. American society tends to understand friendship individualistically and therapeutically, as something done primarily for the improvement of individuals (Bellah, et al., 1985). On this view, friendships are not supposed to be a source of problems, but a means to pleasure and relief and personal betterment. Friendships are a private, individual matter, arising from the spontaneous feelings of the people involved. If the feelings turn bad, many people think the friendship is over. This may make one or both people sad, but nothing important to anyone besides the friends is lost. This way of understanding friendship offers little support for people who need to struggle with power issues in order to maintain their friendship.

Classical and medieval thinkers saw in friendship a way to maturity as a community member. Friendship imposes disciplines worth working to master, both for one's own sake and for the sake of one's community. In his lectures on friendship, Aristotle (1955) identifies friendship as the basis of effective government, as a foundation for practical knowledge of human affairs, and as a realization, a kind of harvest, of individual virtue: people become good in order to be worthy friends. He recognizes that "The wish for friendship develops rapidly, but friendship does not." (p. 264) and says that people must spend time together, over time, to develop knowledge and trust. He measures friendship in terms of the number of meals people eat together, allowing that friends will not know each other well until they have eaten a bushel-and-a-half of salt together.

Ailred, Abbot of Rievaulx in the mid-twelfth century, finds in friendship a way to strengthen a whole community, and a way to deepen spirituality by directly experiencing, through moments in the friendship, an image of the divine. Thus he sees friendship as worth working at and teaching about -once one has experience of friendship to draw on. He distinguishes childish friendship, which is based on calculation of mutual advantage or a fantasy of the friend's perfection, from mature friendship. Mature friendship begins when the friends live through disillusionment with one another. Ailred teaches that an extended period of what he calls "probation" is an essential stage of mature friendship. In this stage, friends test one another to try the other's trust. One result of this testing is that a friend can perform one of the central duties of friendship: giving criticism which upholds the ideals that the friends share in the context of mutual respect and affection. Ailred counsels that friendship should not be dissolved lightly, but only because of betrayal of the friendship itself.

These ideas seem a bit odd to people accustomed to thinking about friendship in individualistic terms, but they provide a corrective for some of the negative effects of individualism on friendships. Ailred's idea is that older people in a community have a duty to instruct younger people in friendship first by example, but also by providing advice, encouragement, and teaching, and by insisting that the whole community work to achieve the civility necessary to support friends as they struggle. Aristotle's idea is that friendship isn't just a private matter between individuals, but that the positive effects of friends working to stay together for the long haul are a key resource to the whole community. Most of us don't live in a physically small world like the Athenian polis or the Cistercian monastery, and most of us wouldn't want to, but the men who formed these places have some important lessons for people trying to make friends today. If we think about what they have to say, we will remember. Friendship is not just spontaneous; it is intentional, involving duties and virtues that are worth working to develop. Friendship is not just for the self-improvement of individuals, it contributes to the good of a community.

The context of community

Friendships between people with and without disabilities are unlikely alliances, not because people are unable to attract and enjoy one another, but because of difficulties imposed on making and keeping relationships by the social construction of developmental disability. Dealing with the consequences of beliefs that justify the social exclusion and therapeutic control of people with developmental disabilities is far more than a two person job. To survive effectively in a fragmented society with little room for people with developmental disabilities, friends need to make a conscious choice to situate their friendship within a community of resistance.

A community of resistance is simply a group of people who, among other shared interests, recognize the negative effects of common beliefs and practices on their friendships and their friends, and support one another to get on with their lives. They contradict the notion that friendships must be purely private, exclusive, and only one to one (Hunt, 1991).

Judith Snow, Jack Pearpoint, and Marsha Forest sustain their fourteen year friendship by reaching out to include people in their friendship (see Pearpoint, 1990). They purposely seek people who join them in celebrating diversity and thus counter the notion that there is something odd or saintly about them. They purposely seek people who will join them to fight the injustice of systems that divide and violate people. They purposely seek people they can have a good time with. Their friendships are not compartmentalized, and separated from the rest of their lives, but complex, and mixed-up with their whole lives. Each is friends with the other, and each has other friends, but their constellation of friendships is more than permutations of one-to-one relationships. The power of such a complex web of friendships can be considerable: it has sustained Judith's system of personal assistance against repeated bureaucratic attempts to standardize her out of existence; it has energized a large network of people committed to inclusive education; it has supported Jack and Marsha in their transition from ordinary job roles to the uncertainties of working freelance for social change; and, it has given them all a good deal of pleasure.

A community of resistance creates and gives life to a story that counters the dominant social beliefs that devalue the community's members and their relationships (Welch, 1990). This story relieves its members of the debilitating fear that there is something crazy or foolish about their friendship. As the lore grows about how its members have responded to challenges, the community's story guides and sustains action.

A community of resistance contains the hurts of its members, hurts that are too big for two individuals to hold between themselves alone. If it is to sustain real people, such a community cannot promise to fix its members or magically remove their pains with some technique. Indeed, Jean Vanier points out that community develops out of people's willingness to walk with one another in their shared weakness as well as their strength.

> *Community is the place where are revealed all the darkness and anger, jealousies and rivalry hidden in our hearts (Vanier, 1992, p. 29).*

People don't need to be perfect to hold one another's hurts, they simply need to be willing to listen, to look for ways to act together when action makes sense, and to find ways to bear with each other when action doesn't help.

In the context of a community of resistance, people will be able to deepen the attraction that draws them together, regardless of disability; they will be able to work against the barriers to embodying their friendships; and they will be able to struggle creatively with the power issues that arise around and between them. By so doing, they will contribute to a modest revolution, built of the daily activities of people who are unlikely allies against the beliefs and practices that make friendships difficult. As the community of resistance to separation of people with developmental disabilities grows, more people will be able to realize the promise of meeting the challenge posed by Robert Williams (1989, p. 19), as he speaks on behalf of the people he has come to know in his work as an advocate with people in institutions.

* * *

Look deep,
deep into the hearts of
my people:
Witness their horror,
Witness their pain.
Horror and pain
your spoken words alone
will never soothe.
Do not try to explain it away,
they will never believe you...
Gallant and gaunt, their beauty.
Beauty,
your spoken words can never
capture.

A perspective on community building

"There's a delicacy about her..."

Five commitments that build community

The importance of community building

Tensions in community building

Unfolding Capacity

The basis of people's lives with one another is twofold, and it is one -the wish of each person to be confirmed as what each person is, even as what that person can become; and the innate capacity in each person to confirm others in this way. That this capacity lies so immeasurably fallow constitutes the real weakness and questionableness of the human race; actual humanity exists only where this capacity unfolds.

-Martin Buber

Three kinds of change, occurring at different scales, shape the opportunities for people with developmental disabilities to participate in unfolding the capacity for mutual confirmation which Buber places at the heart of humanity.

- At the scale of nations, declarations of social policy, such as the *UN Standard Rules on the Equalisation of Opportunities for Persons with Disabilities*, the Canadian Constitution's Charter of Rights and Freedoms and the Americans With Disabilities Act, reflect a new awareness of the rights (and political influence) of people with disabilities and their families by forbidding discrimination on the basis of disability.
- Services to people with developmental disabilities gradually shift attention and investment away from congregate services. So small but growing and visible numbers of people with substantial disabilities live in ordinary housing, have support for ordinary employment, and attend ordinary schools.
- At the smallest scale are the efforts that concern this chapter. This kind of change involves people learning together how to build community across the imposed social barriers that separate people with substantial disabilities from other people.

Each of these changes serves as a platform for further change by revealing how much more must be done before people with substantial disabilities take their rightful place as citizens. Even where they are in force, declarations of rights serve as much to expose contradictions with other policies, and conflicts with other political interests, as they do to stimulate habitual regard for the dignity of people with disabilities. The successes of people with substantial disabilities in living, working, and learning in ordinary places increase dissatisfaction at the contrast between their situation and the far less satisfactory conditions still imposed on many people who remain segregated and controlled by the service programs they rely on. These successes also yield disappointment because establishing people in typical settings seldom proves sufficient to support full and valued lives. More and more people who have worked hard for service reform nod a bit sadly when someone observes that people with disabilities are in communities without yet belonging to communities. Work to build community remains very small in scope, with many more people debating it than people working to learn how to do it.

A perspective on community building

This chapter offers a perspective on efforts to build community. In general terms, we can define community building as...

...the intentional creation of relationships and social structures, that...

...extend the possibilities for shared identity and common action among people...

... outside usual patterns of economic and administrative interaction.

We are especially interested when this work involves people with developmental disabilities.

In particular, this chapter presents some of what we have learned by listening to the stories of people who have made important changes in their lives by working together. Our method for learning is simple: we locate people with developmental disabilities who have been involved in an important change, ask involved people to tell us their stories of how the change happened, invite their reflections on what was most important in making the change, look for common images and themes across stories of change, re-read the stories through different theoretical lenses, and, finally, re-tell the story and ask the original story tellers to correct or extend our account of the changes they have made. Clearly this method does not produce singular techniques or manuals of procedure for community building. Instead, it offers multiple ways to conceive action. (For complementary, but different, reading of the lessons in some of these same stories see Mount, 1991 and the first two chapters of this book).

The changes we have learned from include: establishing adequate support for family life; moving from an institution, medical hospital, nursing home, or group residence into one's own home; moving from one's family's home to a home of one's own; getting a job in an ordinary community workplace; and attending primary, secondary, or tertiary school as a member of ordinary classes. Because all of the people we learned from have developmental disabilities, these changes have each required negotiating entry into new settings and new roles, usually as the first person with a developmental disability to do so; arranging adequate systems of personal assistance; acquiring appropriate technical aids and devices; and finding adequate funding.

These important personal changes have additional significance because none of them resulted from the routine operation of the human service programs available to the people involved. While people who work in services often play an important role in these stories of change, their contributions lie well outside their job descriptions and often challenge their employer's expectations. While money allocated for services usually contributes to making or sustaining the change, people have always had to work to change the established use of these funds, and sometimes have had to create new agencies, or even new policies and laws to make the change they seek.

Of course, these are not the only possible stories of community building. Some service agencies, and a few authorities responsible for service systems, have invested in learning how to routinely offer assistance in ways that make it less difficult for the people they assist to build community. But the changes we want to learn from here take service system resources into a different social space, a social space created around and with a particular person, and among people who discover new commitments and new ways to act through their shared effort. This context reshapes the usual functions and processes of service in ways which yield creative responses to common problems and important lessons for service reformers.

A brief sketch of a story of positive change provides a basis for a description of five types of person to person commitments. People involved in the work of community building have found these terms of description useful in understanding and extending their efforts.

"There's a delicacy about her..."

This phrase, "There's a delicacy about her", captures an aspect of Lisa which was not apparent to the people who lived and worked with her during the years that she moved from one residential facility to another and another and another. In those settings, her inabilities, primarily her inability to use words, and her challenging behaviors defined her person and her life. She was moved from place to place as one service agency after another concluded that she was too difficult to serve. Through these hard years, Lisa's mother, Gemma, remained a fierce advocate for appropriate services, providing Lisa with a firm anchor in a turbulent and threatening world. (This sketch of Lisa's story is drawn from Joyce, 1993.)

As Lisa faced yet another transfer from an institutional setting which had proven dangerous to Lisa, Gemma and Lisa found a committed assistant in John, an official in the regional bureaucracy that oversees services to people with disabilities. John decided that he wanted to respond to the growing political pressure around Lisa by developing individualized services for her. With Gemma's consent, John assigned Marilyn to design and develop services for Lisa. In the ensuing eight years Marilyn has proven herself as one of Lisa's strongest allies, though her job and family circumstances have changed several times.

Marilyn approached Lisa and Gemma with the image of a social structure in mind, an image transmitted from the experience of Judith Snow and her circle of friends as they developed individual supports for Judith (Pearpoint, 1990). Marilyn says,

> *Once I would have asked, "What can I bring to Lisa?" But, instead, I asked, "***Who*** can I bring to Lisa." ...I introduced the idea to Gemma by saying that I thought we needed more people... (p. 3, emphasis in original).*

Gemma consented, but she remembers,

> *[Marilyn] described a circle where Lisa would have people around her who'd care. I didn't think it would ever happen. I though she was asking too much of herself and others. At first I was rather skeptical; I didn't think people would come through with their commitments. I didn't believe a support circle could happen -but it has! (p. 4).*

The support circle hasn't just happened. It developed initially from Marilyn's invitations to people she knew. Then, as action with and around Lisa grew, some people brought in others, like

Elinore (the first person Marilyn invited) who involved her husband, Charlie, and then her daughter Lynne, who later became a key paid assistant to Lisa. As Marilyn continued to act outside Gemma's expectations of a service worker, the circle grew stronger. Gemma says,

> *...I began to trust Marilyn because I saw her as a leader -she's determined and what she sets out to do she does. It's amazing to me that she brought in her friends. (5)*

Since its beginning, the circle has offered Lisa's brothers, Michael and Antosh, a specific focus for their desire to anchor their sister's future. The circle's early work was difficult, especially because no service providers were willing to offer individualized supports, even though Lisa had access to developmental amounts of funding. Michael says,

> *...The meetings were long, and there were lots of frustrations... A lot of the professionals were willing to listen and give advice, but few were willing to get their hands dirty or commit fully. (p. 6)*

Antosh identifies the continuing concern of those closest to Lisa,

> *I was afraid the circle would break down, that it would be too much of a burden. (6)*

Dealing over time with the complexities of developing and maintaining good assistance for Lisa, as well as the challenge of understanding and clarifying Lisa's interests and capacities and finding opportunities for her, has been challenging. So, the circle's growth has not been smooth nor has its membership been stable. When an agency agreed to organize services for Lisa, many circle members assumed that the problem was solved and became less active. At one point, only three people were regularly involved.

However, as continuing problems clarified the fact that individualized services for Lisa posed too big a challenge to the culture of the only existing agency willing to serve her, the circle regenerated and enlarged. Members of Lisa's circle joined with several families whose dreams and desires outstripped the service system's capacity. They formed an association which has created a service agency called New Frontiers, whose mission is to assist a small number people with substantial disabilities as they take their rightful place in their local community.

After eight years, 28 people identified themselves as members of Lisa's circle. Some were introduced to Lisa by other circle members. Some initially met Lisa when they were hired to work for her as assistants (though many of Lisa's assistants have not identified themselves as members of the circle). Some have come to her through the shared work of creating New Frontiers.

Circle members do much more than have planning meetings, and some members rarely attend the meetings that do occur. But each member identifies her or himself with Lisa and with the circle, each shares some mutually interesting activities with Lisa, and all have shown their willingness to act together to protect Lisa and promote a positive future for her. Lisa benefits from the many different ways in which people have come to know her, even though these differences have sometimes caused conflicts among circle members.

The circle benefits each of its members, though it holds Lisa at its center. The circle manifests social concern to reshape its member's community; it is not an expression of pity for disability. All members can identify benefits from membership, including: discovering new skills, making friends, overcoming stereotypes, joining in enjoyable social activities, gaining confidence in ability to problem solve, finding opportunities to act vigorously on what seems right, finding support in personal hard times, and creating confirmation of hope that people can work together to make a real difference.

With the support of the circle and the assistance of New Frontiers, Lisa's life in her home is gradually becoming more stable overall, though some of her behavioral challenges persist, and she remains unable to use words to communicate. Lisa explores the places and activities available in her city. She regularly volunteers her time to Meals on Wheels and to a local community centre. She particularly enjoys many of the meals and parties that embody the life of the circle. Through the shared work that builds and sustains the circle, she and her mother have gained many allies concerned for her future. One of them, Jennifer, says,

> *It's one thing to think about how far Lisa has come -I think more about where Lisa can go. (p. 34)*

Herb, a psychologist who has visited Lisa and encouraged her circle, says,

> *...whenever I have been to Lisa's home or talked to the people who are in her circle, I have been struck by how much they love her and one another. Not in the everything-is-beautiful kind of way that has a hard time with conflict, but in the enduring, patient, and respectful way we all need, to get to the next and better version of ourselves. (20)*

Five commitments that build community

As we have come to understand it, community building happens when people step outside the roles prescribed by the formal and informal administrative structures and assumptions that typically organize life for people with developmental disabilities. Distinctions between staff and clients and family members and ordinary citizens dissolve as the familiar patterns of interaction that maintain them shift, and people discover new possibilities for shared action. This dissolution of administratively fundamental distinctions can be confusing and threatening, especially when people continue to fill administratively prescribed roles.

This confusion shows up in many ways, for example in debates about whether or not paid staff can be friends and advocates for people with developmental disabilities. Many who say yes seem to think that staff can presume that their clients will see them as friends and advocates, despite fundamental inequalities in power, and professional norms that dictate objectivity and detachment. Some, who have glimpsed the bureaucratic machinery beneath the mask of professionalized caring, say no, paid people can't be friends. Neither those who say yes nor those who say no seem to have adequate terms to describe the relationships that have developed between Lisa and Gemma and some paid staff people. Finding new terms outside the usual administrative vocabulary allows people to discuss some of the distinctions that emerge when people work together to make change. New words offer one way to help people make sense of this different way of acting.

Community building is an intentional move into a new space; if Marilyn had chosen to focus on what services to give Lisa rather than on who to bring into her life, the support circle would not exist. Far more an improvisation in response to changing circumstances than a carefully choreographed routine, community building needs ways of identifying the kinds of actions that can make positive differences to people's shared future. Invitation lies at the heart of community building and shapes the responses people offer. Searching for ways to communicate the different kinds of contributions that people can make to one another offers those who make invitations a vocabulary for considering their options.

As we have considered the differences between stories, like Lisa's, that include positive changes and stories that do not, as yet, include much change, we have labeled five different person to person commitments, which are identified on the figure below. In stories of change, we can usually identify people enacting these different commitments. In stories where no change has occurred, the absence of people making one or more of these commitments is notable. This does not mean that no change can happen without each commitment, only that significant change will require even more effort in the absence of one or more of them. When we describe these commitments to people who appear to display them, the people involved usually accept the description as more or less accurate for them, though they sometimes say that the words we have chosen seem a bit strange. So these descriptions have heuristic rather than predictive or technical value.

The notion of commitment involves accepting a particular kind of responsibility by acting on it. One person can share more than one commitment with a person with a developmental disability. Commitment implies freedom; the roles assigned to people by administrative structures do not contain, nor can they compel, any of these commitments. Someone may be both a paid staff person and an ally, as Marilyn has been for Lisa. But John, as Marilyn's boss, can not assign her to be Lisa's ally, though John could, as a person Marilyn respects because of his willingness to take personal risks on Lisa's behalf, invite and encourage her to consider alliance. Commitments are not disability specific; they seem necessary in any effort to build community. People with disabilities can, of course, enact any of the commitments, just as people without disabilities can. These commitments are a matter of one's heart's desire, than of status or apparent skill.

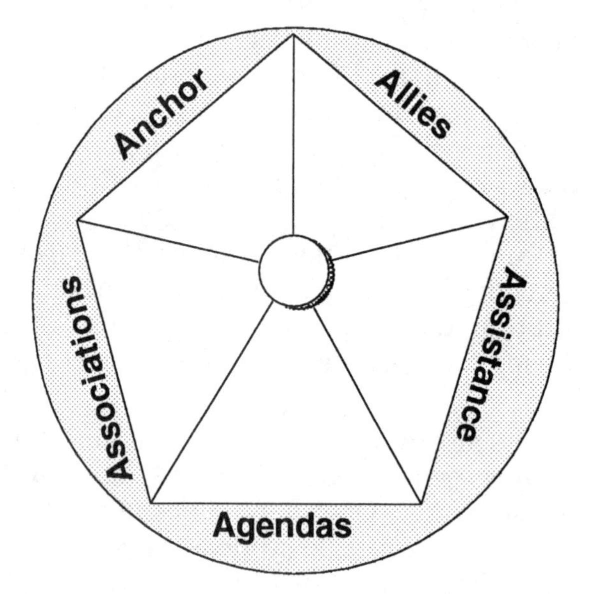

People who commit to **anchor** another person love that person and are concerned with that person's well being over time. They share their life with the person and act as a source of continuity for the person through the ups and downs of life; they have custody of important memories. They stand with the person in difficult times. They act vigorously to protect the person from harm. They seek ways to reconcile with the person when the person has offended them or when they have fallen out with the person. They want to continually grow in knowledge of the person, and especially of the person's gifts and capacities, even though this may be difficult when it challenges habitual patterns of expectation. They work to identify and create opportunities for the person. The other person figures in their decision's about their lives; when facing an important choice they will not need to be reminded of their importance to the person. They actively assist the person to expand relationships with others who may come to care.

People's family members may be anchors, as Gemma is for Lisa. But some family members can be overwhelmed by their own circumstances or by fear or by stereotyped thinking and be unable to anchor their son or daughter or brother or sister or spouse in making the kind of change that builds community. Unrelated people -including paid staff- can find themselves loving a person with a developmental disability in this way, though this can be confusing and difficult for others to understand and can create significant conflicts for the staff person who is an anchor.

People who commit themselves to be **allies** share their time and resources with the person to make a jointly meaningful change. They offer practical help, assist with scheming and problem solving, lend experience and skills, and offer useful information. They make contacts for one another and bring others into the alliance. They usually enjoy the person's company in some mutual interest, and they often like to share food and drink. Because allies know the person in distinct ways, they come to have important knowledge of the person's interests and capacities. On the basis of this information, and their knowledge of community opportunities, they can join the person and the person's anchors to define a future worth working towards. Allies may be linked more closely to the person than they are to one another. If a shared project calls on them to work together, allies may have to deal with their differences with one another and be willing to negotiate conflicts instead of just walking away.

A person's allies may choose to consciously form a circle, as Lisa's have, or their relationship may be more like separate spokes related to the person, with no rim linking them together. Because many people with developmental disabilities have been isolated and separated by prejudiced treatment, it may be necessary to purposely invite people to consider forming alliances with them around an important change, as Marilyn did when she formed a circle around developing individualized supports for Lisa.

Assistance provides the help a person requires to deal with the effects of disability so that they contribute their gifts to the change effort. Service managers offer assistance, as John did for Lisa, when they allocate funds with the flexibility to allow involved people design and re-design a system of everyday personal assistance. Personal assistants provide necessary help with daily activities, from eating and dressing and housework to working and participating in community activities. Professional assistants offer specialized help to deal with difficulties in movement or communication, or learning, or problem solving, or dealing with problematic behaviors or feelings.

The particular commitment of assistance is to offer necessary help, in a respectful, creative, and flexible way, without taking over the persons life. The art is to assist without intruding between the person and other people or activities the person wants to be involved with. The gift of assistance is to resonate with and thus to amplify the person's bodily and mental contributions to the change effort.

Assistants can, of course, become deeply involved with the people they help: many of Lisa's allies have worked for her. But the commitment to the paradox of assisting without intruding or controlling remains a unique contribution, and it is important that assistants be clear when it is time for them to make it. (Adler, 1993).

Some people with developmental disabilities rely primarily on family members for the help they need, particularly their mothers and sisters. When publicly funded assistance fails to provide alternatives to care by family members, the person's relationship with caregivers can become deeply constraining for them all. When necessary assistance is only available in settings that segregate and control people, opportunities to make the kind of changes that build community are very limited.

Associations are the social structures groups of people create to further their interests. They may be structured formally or informally. They may be focused on social change or on their members' protection or enjoyment or personal development or other political objectives. They may be organized around the particular interests of people with disabilities, as New Frontiers is, or they may be organized around other community purposes, as the community centre where Lisa volunteers is. People with developmental disabilities have typically been excluded from the benefits and responsibilities of association membership, so a great deal of untapped energy can become available if a person's allies can facilitate their membership in associations that can share and shape the person's interests (see Kretzmann and McKnight, 1993).

Agendas organize political action to insure just and effective public policies and their proper implementation. People with developmental disabilities and their families and allies have often joined political coalitions to work for such changes as: personal assistance services and family support services under the control of users or people close to them; inclusive schooling; necessary assistance for individual employment; safe, accessible, and affordable housing; safe, convenient, and accessible transportation; access to adaptive technology and devices; and adequate cash income without stigma. The coalitions and actions that form around agendas multiply the influence of people and their circles.

People who share these five commitments and nurture them over time are likely to create new ways to build and be a community. Lisa and the support circle around her work slowly and modestly to increase the capacity of people in her city to deal creatively with diversity, to decide justly when prejudice threatens participation in the benefits and responsibilities of citizenship, and to make good use of the public funds appropriated to the service of people with disabilities. Lisa and her allies have contributed direction and hard work to the creation of an innovative agency to assist them in defining and making their contribution to common life. They have claimed a new space for shared action, and thereby expanded possibilities for themselves and for other people with developmental disabilities.

The importance of community building

Community building matters importantly to people who claim the freedom to define and pursue a desirable future in a society whose economic sector threatens to colonize the whole of life. Community building matters particularly to people with developmental disabilities because the modern economy typically assigns them to either be objects of professional work or to be on waiting lists to demonstrate the need for such work. Because this work is bureaucratically organized, people with developmental disabilities are vulnerable to domination by state administrative mechanisms when they receive the services politically intended to relieve their kin from the unpaid work of caring for them. When it is not simply invisible, their economic marginalization and administrative domination is often celebrated as desirable, because people with developmental disabilities are widely perceived as less than fully human and cast into devaluing social roles as objects of pity or charity or menace or dread.

When people with developmental disabilities and their friends work together to build community, they can open a social space in which marginalized people can join people who are insiders to penetrate delusions about disability and uncover shared meaning through joint projects. Within this social space, people whose lives may be dominated by professional definitions of disability can find some relief, and even occasional liberation, from the burdens of full time clienthood. Within this social space, people can unfold the human capacity for confirmation of one another as each is, and as each can become.

Judith Snow (1990), whose emancipation from a chronic care facility occurred through her shared life and work with a circle of support, reflected on the contribution outsiders can make to community building simply from the experience of being an outsider.

> *The gift of surviving and growing through change belongs to the outcast... Living on the edge of chaos changes the people who survive it. You become very aware of the value of things ordinary citizens take for granted; things like having your opinion listened to, having a chance to make a mistake, to be forgiven and to have a chance to try again; things like having friends and family who celebrate holidays with you and who will tell their friends that you are looking for a job. Living on the margin either burns you out and kills you, or it turns you into a dreamer, someone who really knows what sort of change will help and who can just about taste it; someone who is prepared to do anything to bring about change. If these dreamers are liberated, if they are brought back into the arms of society, they become the architects of the new community; a community that has a new capacity to support everyone's needs and interactions. But how can this really be, especially since these dreamers still have the characteristics that marked them as outcasts in the first place? They will still lack good judgment, or find it hard to learn to read, or be disabled. Solving this problem is critical, for otherwise the outcasts and the ordinaries are very good at maintaining an invisible wall between their two worlds. (pp. 126-127)*

She goes on to say that this invisible wall can only be breached by long term willingness to build new kinds of relationships between those who are reaching out and those who are reaching in. In the five commitments, we have tried to describe the terms of those new relationships.

Tensions in community building

A sort of discomfort surrounds these new relationships and some of the social structures that invite and support them. The very term, community building, reflects the tensions that give rise to this discomfort, and to some frank disagreements. For some people, community does not seem to be something that can be built : community is, spontaneously, or it is not. To speak of building community violates what can, and should, only develop naturally and opens the door to a kind of clumsy, intrusive, and embarrassing social engineering, likely packaged in warm and fuzzy psycho-babble. For others, community isn't worth building because it represents a failed structure for human development, incapable of dealing constructively with human diversity or addressing injustice. To speak of building community distracts from the necessity of living as successful individuals in a cosmopolitan and impersonal society. For still others, whether it is desirable or undesirable, the very possibility of community is gone. On their view, the turbulent forces that fragment our times replace community with cleverly marketed counterfeits, like "Community Care," which masks impersonal rationing by joining two words with high appeal, emptying them of content, and filling the hollowed out space with bureaucratic professional activity. To speak of building community is to be guilty of a kind of naive and dangerous flashback to the 1960's or the 1780's.

Awareness of each of these disagreements and discomforts clarifies the work of community building. The economic and administrative forces that shape so much of modern life make it necessary to undertake conscious efforts to claim common spaces and to build within them. And conscious efforts can be and feel halting, tentative, uncertain, and uncomfortable. Recognizing and honoring human diversity and enriching joint action with differing gifts presents so large a challenge that no one who sets out to build community will get far before encountering its threats and frustrations. Efforts to build community that overcome the invisible walls between outsiders and ordinaries must be modest in scale and in expectation.

This kind of building is nothing like the massive imposition of individual will on masses of people through architectural technology which Ayn Rand characterizes in *The Fountainhead.* It is much more like the kind of building celebrated by Bernard Rudofsky (1964) in *Architecture without Architects.* As Rudofsky beautifully illustrates, this kind of building is vernacular rather than formal; commonly practiced by inhabitants rather than sketched and controlled by professional experts who will not live within the results; rooted in a particular landscape rather than imposed upon it; purposely created for human comfort rather than scaled for mass consumption; and built in stages as use and resources expand rather than master planned and financed at high cost. He notes two inspiring qualities of successful vernacular builders: they work to make oases of public spaces, and,

> *...they do not hesitate to seek out the most complicated configurations in the landscape [often choosing] veritable eyries for their building sites... (p. 4).*

A Note on the Linguistic Roots of Friendship

If you want to stand up for a word, it's good to know how deep its roots go, where it comes from, and what it's relations are. Renewing the meaning of old words brings power and richness to life. Deep roots connect people who call one another friend with some of humankind's highest hopes and powers. However flimsy "just friends" may seem in a high-tech world, the expression resonates through ages.

Friend is a word as old as written English. *The Oxford English Dictionary* tells that more than a thousand years ago, the poet sang of Beowulf, who fought the monsters that threatened Hrothgar's household because Hrothgar was Beowulf's friend: "one joined to another in mutual benevolence and intimacy."

At it's beginning, the word friend was created by a contraction of the Old English verb, *frijon,* which means "to love." (Partridge, 1983)

That word in turn arose from an ancient Indo-European root, *prai,* which means "beloved, precious, at peace with, and free." (Shipley, 1984) Powerful ancestors indeed.

The roots of the word friend illuminate the source of some of our most prized human qualities. Liberty and citizenship arise linguistically and politically from groups of people who call one another friends. Freedom, however, does not derive from words that speak of being free of something, but from words that speak of belonging to a circle of friends (Benveniste, 1973). And it is ties of affection and belonging that lie at the linguistic roots of oneself. At root, a person only discovers self among friends.

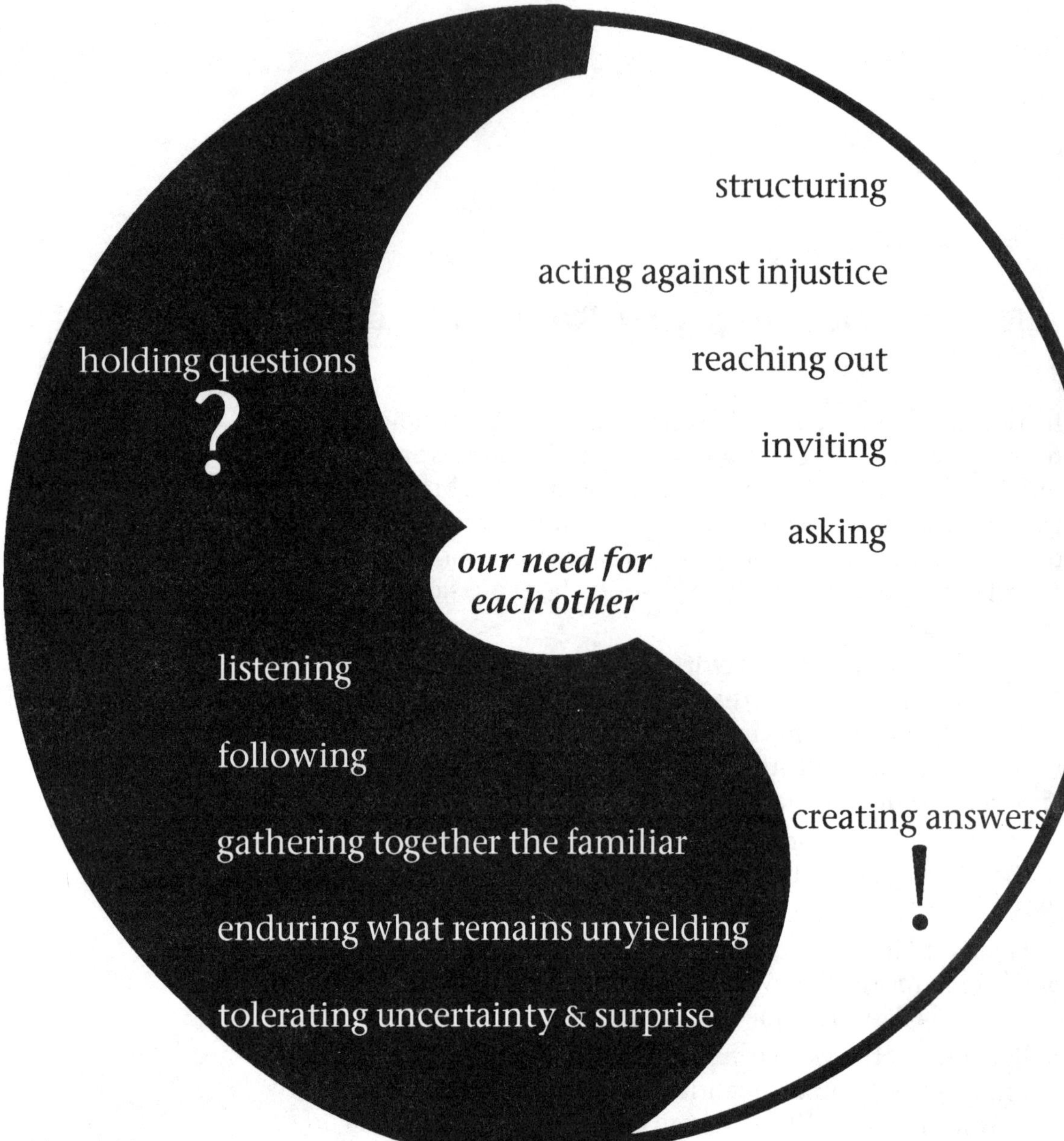

structuring

acting against injustice

holding questions

reaching out

?

inviting

asking

our need for each other

listening

following

creating answers

gathering together the familiar

!

enduring what remains unyielding

tolerating uncertainty & surprise

The complementary and creative nature of these polarities can be described by mapping them onto the *Ta Ki* - symbol of the balance of the two great forces of *yin-yang*.

Reflections on Support Circles

Circles arise from consciousness of our great need for each other.

Sometimes circles begin by attaching this need for others firmly to the person in the center: "She is isolated and needs us." Unless this narrow beginning leads to a dawning awareness of interdependence, of our deep reliance on one another for a good life, the circle will turn into a sort of a square. It will become a soulless project about disability which is motivated by pity, or by an abstract desire to perfect an impersonal system for processing deficiencies.

Circles arise from action that grows out of awareness of our great need for each other. The flow of this energy between holding questions and creating answers energizes circles. As the picture on the facing page suggests, circle facilitators work with the flow of energy between at least five sets of poles. On the light side of the circle are processes for creating. On the dark side of the circle are processes for holding. Each process calls for its opposite, and thus the circle is animated.

asking

listening

Circles begin with **asking** people to come together and then **listening** carefully to the life story of the person in the center: past experiences, present realities, and future aspirations. Listening together feelingly, intuitively, thoughtfully, and with each of the senses leads to a shared glimpse of the person's dream: the threads that give this particular life significance and meaning; the threads that animate this person's particular contribution to our common life; the threads that glow when this person is passionately engaged. A glimpse of someone's dream organizes and motivates efforts to help that person to establish the living conditions and develop the opportunities necessary to allow the person's identity to unfold.

Listening leads back to asking: asking circle members to move through fears and uncertainties to say clearly what they most want to create for themselves and for one another; asking one another for commitments to the action steps that will trace a path toward what they most want; asking others for cooperation, for resources, for access to opportunities.

The Support Circle Mentoring Project, which is funded by the Pennsylvania Developmental Disabilities Planning Council, gathered people involved with facilitating circles to share what they are learning. This chapter is a reflection of their thinking.

Asking leads back to listening. What more can we sense, think, feel, and intuit now that we have come this far? What more can we ask?

inviting
following

The circle follows the person in the center by accommodating particular preferences about how this person wants others to listen, and by making agreements about which aspects of how this person wants to live that circle members will work to make happen. **Following** leads to **inviting** out of an honest wish to broaden this person's horizons or an insight into a gift or ability whose possibilities this person may not realize.

Inviting leads back to following as the circle asks: "What does this person make of a new experience?" "What does an opportunity to exercise an unrealized possibility draw out of this person and those this person relies upon?" This move back to listening is especially important when a person is vulnerable to other's impositions -maybe because this person depends on others for assistance, or because this person has very limited experiences and ability to clearly communicate preferences.

reaching out
gathering

Circles **gather** those who know and care about a person within their circumference. As those within the circle gain clarity about their goals, they usually discover the need for additional members. Sometimes they will **reach out** to people from the person in the center's past: lost or estranged family members or friends who have gotten out of touch. Sometimes they will reach out to people with the knowledge, skills, resources, and gifts to help the person at the center build strength, explore an emerging interest, or gain access to a needed opportunity. Circle members may locate these new people among their own families, friends, or acquaintances or they may go looking for them on the person in the center's behalf.

Reaching out leads back to gathering as the members of the circle become scattered into diverse activities, or lose touch with one another, or with the circle's purpose and focus. This can happen when the work becomes hard, or after a success.

impatience
endurance

The circumstances of many people with disabilities cry out for **action against the injustice** that constrains their lives. From childhood, many people with disabilities suffer enforced exclusion from ordinary places, activities, and experiences; arbitrary control that restricts elementary liberty; poor support and second class service; and, too frequently, neglect and abuse. Some circles act directly to confront unjust treatment and demand changed behavior or different services (as when a circle helps a child gain access to an inclusive school experience); others work to help the person in the center to create new circumstances (as when a circle helps someone establish their own home instead of trying to reform a nursing home).

Because many injustices are systemic, and entrenched behind unconscious myths of people's inability and inequality, many changes which seem self-evidently right to circle members turn out to be much more difficult to make than they predict. The ability to **endure what remains unyielding** in the face of even the most disciplined action is fundamental to the continuing life of the circle.

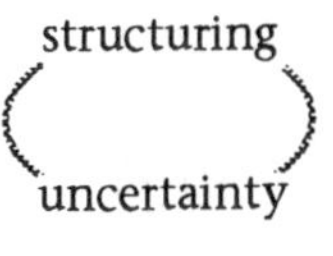

Circle members **create structure** when they set goals, gather and organize information, make and revise plans, construct time lines, accept assignments, and act purposefully to implement their plans. However, circles are not agencies: they don't control staff and budgets that they can deploy to achieve their goals. Their ability to act depends on their ability to enlist cooperation by enrolling people in their vision. Furthermore, the focus of a circle is on the life of the person at the center, not on the completion of a project. New information, new contacts, new experiences, and new relationships can lead to unpredictable changes in direction. So can unexpected barriers and intractable problems.

Structure calls out the capacity to **tolerate uncertainty** and surprise. If circle members need a guarantee that their plans will work before they set out, they will be paralyzed by their lack of formal authority. If circle members judge their efforts solely in terms of objectives achieved on time, they will often be plunged into disappointment. What is wanted is the courage to walk together into uncertainty and the openness to seek new possibilities as things change.

Tolerance of uncertainty and openness to surprise lead back to structure as circle members organize and re-organize around new defeats and new possibilities.

Sustained interdependence calls for many turns into the holding processes to find and re-find direction, to collect and recollect relationships that have become scattered, to discover and rediscover meaning, to sustain and renew energy. The difficulties imposed by the pervasive effects of the social devaluation of people with disabilities make listening, following, gathering, enduring, and tolerating uncertain outcomes particularly important in walking and standing with people with disabilities.

Finding the rhythm

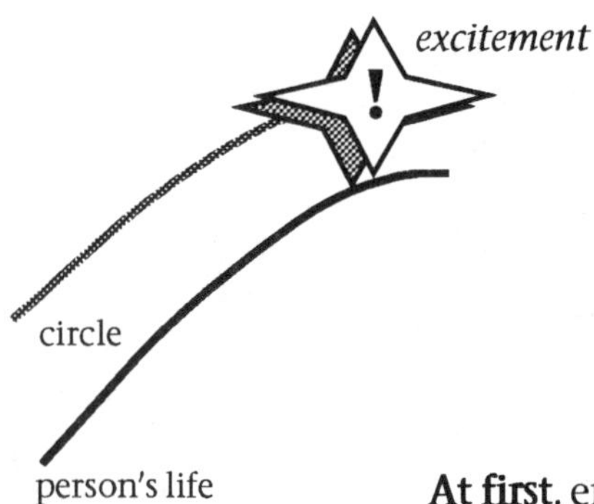

At first, enthusiasm for the circle rises rapidly, as members see the possibility of positive changes for the person at the center and some first steps improve things for the person.

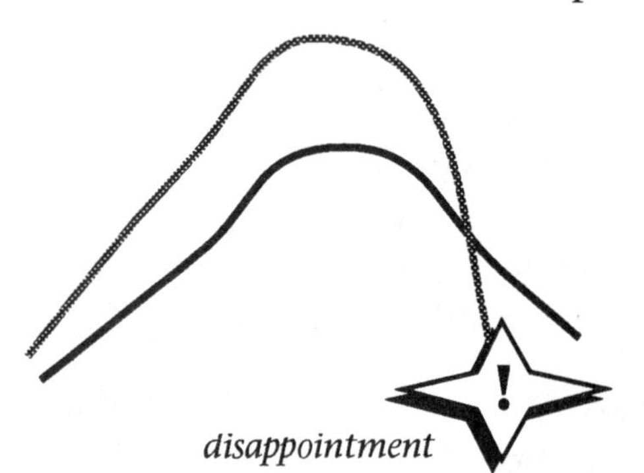

But, a downturn in the person's situation can cause initial enthusiasm for the circle to crash. The same excitement that took circle members up, brings them down as inflated expectations hit real life barriers. Some of the signs of this crash include, circle members feeling...

- Discouraged, "Nothing can really happen."
- Resentful or angry because people who 'should' help refuse to respond as expected or fail to follow through.

circle's rhythm
person's rhythm

- Alone, like "I have to walk up this steep hill all by myself because I'm the only one the person in the center of the circle can really count on."

Our hope is to renew ourselves by seeking a kind of consistency in the life of the circle: highs that aren't so high; lows that aren't so low. As circle members learn to count on each other, the circle can be one source of stability as life goes through its upturns and downturns for the person at the center. This can only happen if circle members learn and practice the arts of renewal...

- Letting our disappointments and our sense of aloneness exist openly between us.
- Offering each other mutual support and encouragement.
- Challenging one another to live up to our commitments and follow through on what we agree to do.
- Sticking with one another in hard times.
- Forgiving and reconciling when members let one another down or offend one another.
- Reaching out to include others who can help.
- Being careful about making final judgements about outcomes. Many good things have come out of -or at least after- discouraging times.
- Remembering the values that brought the circle together and deepening our understanding of them in the shadow of difficult times.
- Celebrating what has happened and the relationships that have grown and endured.

Metaphors for the work of facilitating circles

This work is like...

- Organizing a **quilting bee** -bits and pieces come together through shared efforts... the whole pattern emerges from the vision of a pattern whose final appearance depends on the pieces each person contributes... lots of gossip is exchanged
- **Midwifery** -low tech/high touch support to a natural process... intimate and respectful... a position of services... position and intensity of support varies as needed, based on care-filled listening and watching... competition from others who want to professionalize and mechanize
- **Uncovering** buried treasure; treasure whose value some people will be unable to sense, even when it is uncovered
- **Teaching fearful people to use fire** for heat, light, and uplift (as in filling a hot air balloon) when, out of fear, they want to pour water on the fire
- **Weaving** a spider web
- **Gardening**... planning (and not necessarily following the plans exactly), planting, weeding (and procrastinating about weeding), fertilizing, waiting, harvesting, nourishing, sharing
- Joining a **family**
- Creating **ripples** in a pond by throwing in a stone... or several stones to see the patterns of ripples overlap
- Following in the path of "The Man Who Planted Seeds"
- Riding a **roller coaster** with a loop-the-loop ...thrill and fear are right next to each other
- Being a **juggler** keeping seven plates spinning on top of sticks... but remembering that I don't have to do the act alone -if I ask others to help and make room for them instead of pushing them out of the way
- Being **alone** on a boat in the middle of the ocean (no one I work with seems to get it)
- **Baking brownies** - the recipe says "beat until slightly lumpy"... you can bake all kinds from hard to soft depending on what different people like

Circles and Agency Change

Jay Nolen Community Services in Los Angeles, CA transformed its residential services between 1993 and 1996 by assisting more than sixty people with autism to move from its group homes into their own homes and apartments and then closing its group homes. Circles of support planned and managed each person's transition and maintain responsibility for assuring that people receive adequate services. Their experience provides important insight into the ways circles function when an agency is serious about following their direction.

Circles were an important part of the development of supported living in at least two ways: they provided a forum for decisions about individual supported living arrangements and they gave people a way to contain the anxiety and uncertainty of major change. The requirements of moving have set the circle's agenda. Where should the person live... with whom... with what assistance... how should the place be furnished and decorated? In the period just after the move problems -sometimes big problems- of establishing a household and a support system, and sharing good news about the effects of the move, paced the circle's meetings. These practical issues provided the context for sharing and organizing knowledge about the person's preferences and capabilities and needs and the resources available to the person.

A new constitution

Once a person has moved and things are reasonably stable, the circle needs to re-constitute itself. Its members need to agree on a new constitution by discussing and coming to agreement on these questions:

- What is the purpose of the circle? What contributions does the circle want to make to the life of the person with autism?

- Who is the focus of the circle? This is not as silly a question as it may first appear. Sometimes the actual focus people in a circle are the person's parents in their role as key decision makers and resource people for their son or daughter. If this is so, it should be clear.
- Who belongs to the circle and what are the obligations of membership? The process of moving brought people into the circle as issues arose. Are all of those people circle members; do they want to be active contributors? Does the circle want to have a "reserve list" -people who don't want to be active unless a particular need arises? Are all of the staff involved with the person circle members? If not, who will link the circle's work with them? Are there other people to invite into the circle?
- How does the person with autism participate in the circle?
- If the person has a conservator, how does the conservator see the role of the circle in assisting them with their legal responsibility of making decisions in the person's interest?
- What ground rules does the circle want to adopt, and what skills do its members want to develop, in order to build honest communication, creative problem solving, and the capacity to understand and negotiate conflicts?
- considering these questions, circles should first take time to carefully answer two questions,
- Now that the person lives in his or her own home, what is most important to work on now in order improve the person's life?
- What are our markers and measures that the person is experiencing a good quality of life? What signs will show us that there is a problem we must attend to?

The circle's answers to these questions will provide a foundation for the circle's renewed constitution, so in answering them it is important to think beyond just keeping the person from harm. The skills in personal futures planning and group planning (PATH) that the agency has invested in developing will be helpful to circles in this work.

It will be important for each circle to ask, "How can we adapt the way the circle meets and works to accommodate the person's strongest ways of participating and communicating?"

The politics of circles

Some involved people speak negatively of "politics" in circles. But politics doesn't have to be a negative term. In an important way circle meetings are political meetings: they bring people together who have different points of view and different interests and provide a forum for them to discover common ground and organize shared action. The politics of circles only turn destructive if members are dishonest or manipulative.

One way to make circle politics healthier is to surface important disagreements among circle members. Discussions around a renewed personal futures plan provide a good context for mapping such disagreements. Seven common kinds of disagreements can arise:

- Disagreements about people's vulnerabilities. For example, some people believe that imprecision in administering prescribed medication has severe consequences for a person and others believe that occasional variations in timing or dosage make relatively little difference.
- Disagreements about what staff activities must be performed ("non-negotiables") and what staff practices are optional, depending on circumstances and individual preferences.. For example, some people believe that systematic effort to assist the person to develop friendships is a necessary part of the job; others see this as much less important or even a waste of time because the person with autism is disinterested in friendships.
- Disagreements about a person's strong preferences. For example, some people believe that work matters very much to a person; others believe that the person would rather not work and that the desire is being imposed on the person.
- Disagreements about preferred and reliable methods of communication. Some people believe that a person communicates effectively with facilitated communication; others believe that the person is or was being manipulated by facilitation.
- Disagreements about a person's ability to provide meaningful direction of assistants, regardless of the communication system the person uses.
- Disagreements about how to interpret people's behavior. Some people read a person's difficult behavior as an attempt at manipulation; others read the same behavior as a request for a different sort of relationship.
- Disagreements about how the agency's organizational structure should function: "Who is, or should be, responsible for handling what."

- Disagreements about the future role of the circle and the future responsibility of parents and family members in the person's life. Some people see substantial family involvement as necessary throughout the person's life; others see it as finishing now that the transition is finished.

These disagreements are based on real uncertainties or real differences in perspective; no outside judge or expert can provide a final or objective answer. The circle's obligation is to be clear about the important disagreements they have and explicit about the ways in which they will negotiate these differences. It is not necessary to make an idol of consistency: some disagreements might be resolved by accepting that "when he is with me, this is what happens; when he is with you, that is what happens." Other issues will require negotiation ("How can we discover a way to proceed that will satisfy all of our interests?") or the willing acceptance of authority ("We do it this way because this is the way his mother wants it.") If these disagreements remain unspoken, or if circle members don't accept a common way of dealing with differences, the differences will poison and paralyze the circle.

How you know when your circle isn't round

Before a circle considers what matters most for the person and what it's constitution will be, the circle should take time to review its own functioning. Based on our interviews, we constructed this checklist of potential problems in the functioning of circles:

- Circle members see the circle as belonging to someone else: "We have these meetings because they are important to ________" Staff say, "parents". Parents say, "staff." Anybody says, "We have them because the executive director says we have to."
- Important decisions about a person's life happen without the circle's participation, for example: a circle member says "It's not like we work together or anything" when explaining why someone who is not a circle member is creating a plan for the person the circle supports.
- The circle turns to a pyramid with a parent at the top. Parents review the details of staff performance. Parents feel, "Agency leaders expect us to do what agency supervisors are paid to do." Staff feel, "The parent wants to use me to control every detail of the person's life."
- The circle turns to a pyramid with no one at the top. Staff try to get parents to act like supervisors or representatives of their agenda to JNCS administrators.

- ▲ The circle spends time on activities that would be much more efficiently done in other ways, for example: paying the person's bills, explaining JNCS policies, reviewing the details of staff schedules when there is no major issue at stake.
- ▲ Circle meetings focus mostly on "How things were done" rather than on "What we have learned" and "What it is important for the person for us to do."
- ▲ A parent feels, "I am the only advocate for my daughter or son."
- ▲ Staff people are disengaged during the meeting and feel frustrated or angry after the meeting.
- ▲ The circle gets stuck in polarization: its "staff against parents" or "circle members against support staff" or "administrative team members against support staff", or "outsider parents against insiders on the board."
- ▲ Some circle members treat other circle members is a disrespectful way but the issue is never raised and people do not make amends for the offense.
- ▲ Conversations about circle problems happen outside the circle, in pairs or other groups, and do not result in changes in the way the circle works.
- ▲ The only thing that gets a circle unstuck is when a person in authority (often the executive director or board president) shows up and assumes responsibility for dealing with the problem, perhaps by delegating action to a staff person.

Because circles deal with difficult issues and because their work is organizing action on important issues, all circles will loose their roundness from time to time. This issue is whether the circle has the strength to notice that it is stuck and find a way to get unstuck that makes the circle stronger.

The agency role in making circles stronger

The agency can do several things that will make circles stronger:

- o Invest in training and supervision in facilitation, creative problem solving, conflict negotiation, and personal futures planning for anyone who wants to learn. Assure that each circle has more than one member interested in improving their skills in these critical areas.
- o Identify and share the variety of ways members of different circles have of listening to a person and making decisions about the person's priorities and preferences. Approaches may include: stories about shared experiences, observations on the way a

person responded during a private discussion, rituals that have meaning to the person or in a particular relationship, responses to photographs or drawings, and unconventional methods the person has invented in order to communicate.

- Make facilitators who are not members of a circle available for personal futures planning, PATH, or circle reviews. Facilitators can be members of other circles: staff, family members, others who are interested and willing to get training and supervision.
- Make consultation available to circles that are deeply stuck (what some people call "The Circle Doctor"). The emotional work involved can sometimes overwhelm even capable people. Consultants focus on process rather than having an organizational authority role or a stake in the outcomes of a circle's decisions.
- Find ways to make information about routine agency business available to circle members without taking up circle meeting time.
- Much confusion and conflict comes from lack of clarity about the responsibility of circles, parents, and agency supervisors. Ask each circle to go through a systematic process of identifying responsibility for key tasks. One way to do this is sketched below.
- The agency can gather and share its experience with circles: benefits, disappointments, what has worked, what has not worked as expected, guidelines from experience. *The circle cookbook* might be a nice title.

This process of re-constituting circles should be carried out systematically, for each circle. It should raise a number of important questions whose answers have implications for the agency as a whole:

- Is it acceptable for a person the agency supports to have no circle, either around the person or around the person's parents? If so, how will the planning, decision making, and safeguarding functions of the circle happen for the person?
- Is it acceptable for a person to have a circle when the person's parents do not participate; if the person's conservator does not participate? If so, how will agency respond to conflicts between the person's circle and the person's parent/conservator?
- Is it acceptable to have a circle in which the person with autism does not participate?
- Do staff participate as circle members as an expected part of their job responsibilities or can they choose not to be members of a person's circle? Can a circle exclude a staff member?

Community Building and Supported Living

Options in Community Living in Madison WI is a pioneer in supported living for people with developmental disabilities.

Community building has grown out of a sense of unrealized opportunity in the lives of many of the people Options supports. Success in assisting people to make and keep their own homes gave a number of people the foundation they needed to develop and extend their network of acquaintances and friends and memberships. But a number of people have fewer and shallower connections in Madison's communities than is desirable, given Option's mission and commitment to full citizenship. So, more than ten years ago, Options' staff began work on the question of how to support people in making community connections.

Through the years, Options tried a variety of strategies, each of which confirmed the importance of supporting people's community connections and none of which seemed to go deep enough to make a significant shift in the isolation many people continue to experience. As staff became more convinced of the importance of community connections they became more frustrated by the competition for time and attention between the myriad tasks required to support people in their day to day lives and the work of helping people make community connections. Training and consultation strengthened conviction about the importance of community connections, which increased frustration at limited progress and a sense that Options was letting people down in this important area of their lives. Persistent inability to make time for this work within the jobs of community support workers and team coordinators led Options to separate community building from day to day support and dedicate one staff person's time to the work of community building.

Defining community building as a separate organizational function, and assigning this function to a skilled staff member, has broken through Options' sense of frustration about community connections. Significant changes for the people directly involved in community building generate a different kind of news about what Options can assist the people it supports to accomplish.

Signs of accomplishment

Three kinds of changes signal the benefits of Options' concentration on community building as a distinct activity.

The people with disabilities involved have seen important improvements in their lives. They have had the experience of being at the focus of intense and careful listening aimed at discovering what they are interested in, who and what they might benefit from getting to know, and what accommodations are necessary to allow their participation. Other people have worked thoughtfully to smooth their path into new places. They have had company in trying new experiences; some of these have lasted and led to new activities and relationships, and some have led nowhere in particular. Their experiences have interested, gratified -and sometimes even inspired- some members of their families and some of the staff who know them. People who know them say that they have grown in their confidence and knowledge of their own interests, wants, and ability to contribute.

Some people in community settings have gotten to know, participate with, and sometimes to care about a person whose apparent differences might have otherwise been a barrier to their involvement. Community members have expanded their sense of hospitality a bit and made some accommodations to support involvement. Some of them report a paradoxical insight: disability, even when it involves substantial differences in communication, is no big deal.

Staff at Options have increased their expectations for the people they support, gotten to know people in new ways because they are having different experiences, and strengthened their understanding of Options' mission. Some staff have developed new skills and confidence.

It is interesting to notice that over the years a number of the people Options supports have found familiar places, joined in community activities, and formed good new relationships, and a number of Options staff have facilitated people's community involvement. A good measure of this happened before the community building initiative got under way, and a number of staff continue to encourage and assist new connections. What seems to make the accomplishments of people currently involved in community building important is their unpredictability. What has happened was hard to predict because previous assumptions...

... about the person led others to believe that the person would be disinterested in activities and relationships that have proven rewarding to the person. ("I never would have thought that (s)he would...")

...about "the community" led others to believe that the person would not be welcome in a place or relationship that has proven hospitable. ("I never would have thought that they would accept him or her.")

Reflection on the first of these interrupted assumptions -the person won't want to- underlines the central place of active invitation in community building. The process is not one of checking what a person says they want and then hunting for it in the community. It often seems to be a process of accompanying , encouraging, and directly assisting the person to discover interests and possibilities by trying things with someone who gives them (or perhaps others important to them) a sense of safety and confidence. Asked if they knew what they wanted to do before they got involved with community building, people answered, "No." No one who has learned the lessons of this work will ever again say, "We asked, but there is really nothing the person wants to do."

Success factors

The success of this strategy to date seems to depend on four critical factors:

- Options staff do a good job of supporting people in their daily lives. Everyday tasks get done, people get the assistance they need, and staff work hard on the inevitable problems that arise to threaten the effectiveness of people's support systems. Community support workers want the people they support to have genuine connections to their communities. The overall good quality of support provides people with a strong base from which to pursue their interests in community.
- The person responsible, Kathryn Mazack, has earned credibility by exemplifying Options' values as she worked successfully in different roles over the years of her employment. Other Options leaders see her as working from her heart and bringing strong gifts of intuition to her decision making. Kathryn feels and communicates a passionate commitment to helping people

build good relationships. The challenge of learning about conscious community building seems to have a deep resonance with her own personal development; her challenges at work and her present stage in her own life's journey seem to energize each other. Probably because of this resonance, Kathryn was ready and willing to stretch herself to work in new ways, in new places, and with new people.

- The availability of an experienced consultant, Kathy Bartholomew-Lorimer, who had the trust of key Options staff because she combines deep commitment to shared values with practical knowledge of how to make community connections and skill in supporting staff development. Kathy's approach to planning with people and building personal community connections provides a template for this work.
- The budgetary flexibility to differentiate community building as a specific form of support that Options offers to some of the people it serves which allowed the creation of a specific role for a community builder.

Defining community building

Options two years of work with community building allows a formal definition to emerge that distinguishes community building from many other important things that Options staff do and outlines an agenda for further learning.

> **Community building is** the way Options staff learn about purposefully forming and organizing relationships, based on an emerging plan which captures a person's desire to explore and develop new memberships and relationships. Community building is focused on extending a person's opportunities to contribute to mutual relationships and is consciously oriented toward building the habits and skills of welcome in community settings.

The idea of formally defining community building only after two years of doing it might seem odd, but it reflects the way Options typically innovates. This approach, which might seem backwards from the point of view of linear problem solving, fits community building particularly well because it begins with action on behalf of individuals. While each person involved in community building could be understood as starting in the same place (all seemed isolated from Madison's communities in an important way), each has ended up with very different connections which have developed in somewhat different ways. This inductive approach to defining community building is very different from the way others have approached the reality of people's isolation. Citizen advocacy, for example, was exhaustively formally defined before it was tried; its practitioners work to figure out how to implement a prior definition.

This more formal definition offers a safeguard against superficial approaches by acknowledging that community building means more than helping people with disabilities fill their schedules with activities. It recognizes that community building means more than simply responding to what a person says they want to do. Those involved in community building expect the person to discover a greater capacity to provide leadership in their own life by participating in a planning process and by searching for ways to contribute to community life. It reminds the community builder that her work is not to leave community settings as she finds them, but to act as a leaven for small but important changes in community associations.

Thinking about community building from the point of view of this definition makes it three dimensional, as the following diagram suggests.

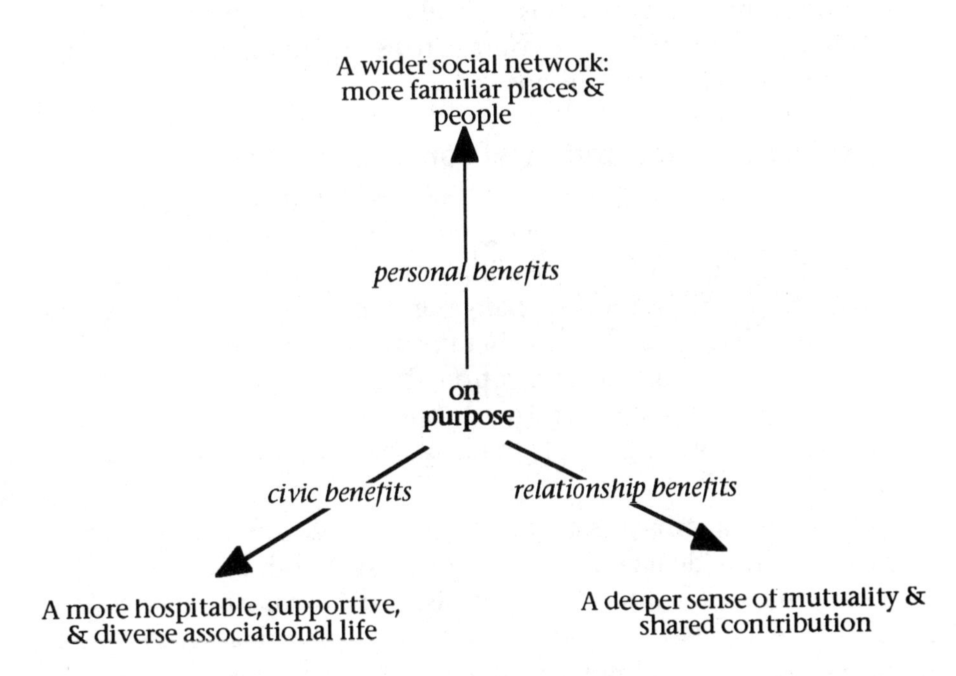

This three dimensional diagram suggests that the community builder purposely works with three distinct good things in view. She looks for ways to positively influence both the person and the community members the person meets by increasing their awareness of joint interests: the possibility for common purpose and shared action that redefines the social boundaries that have excluded people. While taking opportunities to move along any one of the three lines, she remembers that the point is to move along all three. She remembers the whole thing she is working to shift. Having more places to go where people know your name is a good thing, but it is not the whole thing. Increasing the diversity of an association's membership roster is a good thing, but it is not the whole thing. Giving of your energy and talents is a good thing, but it is not the whole thing.

One vital part of the community builder's work involves clarifying purpose by asking both the person with a disability and people in community settings two kinds of questions. The first kind of questions increases awareness of purpose and interests (*What is important to you?*); the second kind of questions stimulates exchange and shared action (*What do you want to do about it together?*). Part of the art of community building is creating the kind of conversation in which it is fruitful to ask these questions; one of its challenges is finding the courage to ask them forthrightly and listen imaginatively to the answers.

Clarifying understanding of community

Two different ways of understanding community emerge on reflection. One understanding seems more psychological. It stresses individual choice, personal fulfillment, individual choice and satisfaction, symmetrical exchange, and spontaneously arising and declining relationships. The other understanding seems more moral.* It stresses mutual obligation, the rewards of shared responsibility for taking care of and contributing to each other, and the importance of calling people to recognize, fulfill, and stick with their obligations.

These two approaches are not exclusive: today, people need to make an individual choice to recognize their obligation to the common good; and accepting the discipline of faithful service to each other can be a deep source of personal growth and fulfillment. But community building seems to lose its edge if it loses the authority and conviction that comes from a moral understanding of community.

* This is an uncomfortable choice of words, but a better one doesn't come to mind. If the connotations of the word "moral" in these paragraphs are a barrier, try "ethical" or maybe even "political" instead. We didn't use them because we didn't want to suggest that a psychological understanding of community was not an ethical or political one. Of course this has nothing to do with lording it over people and dictating the details of their conduct; it is about recognizing that these are issues of right and wrong and that right lies in the direction of greater inclusion and greater mutual responsibility, whatever that may turn out to be.

A different kind of asking happens when the community builder is thinking psychologically about common interests in terms of natural compatibility and balance of individual rewards than happens when the community builder is thinking about the importance of helping people notice opportunities to honor their personal and civic obligations to one another. As Tom Kohler put it, describing his work as a citizen advocacy coordinator,

> *"I believe that there is a deep crack in the world and that vulnerable people will fall into that crack. It's my job to ask people to do what it takes to keep that from happening to each other."*

Signs of Community Building

Beyond intellectual concern for the possibility of community, some people work to enact it through their choice of living and working arrangements. Compared to the forces driving people toward individualism, their efforts seem small, partial, risky, and hopeful. Chester County, PA benefits from several quiet initiatives generated by the long term work of such hopeful people, who have created...

...A community garden, in which families from a wide area buy shares to support the gardeners in return for a share of the produce.

...A law practice dedicated to assisting people to make good and enduring agreements and to preventing and constructively mediating conflicts.

...Several bio-dynamic farms — whose farmers are committed to restoring and maintaining the living soil as a sustainable source of organic, pesticide free food— and their associated distribution systems: a natural yoghurt company, operated cooperatively, which distributes the produce of one of the farms and operates a store; a bakery: and a milk distribution operation. These farms also teach their farming methods to apprentices.

...Two very different intentional communities which include members with disabilities and serve as the focus for a variety of cultural activities as well as shared households and shared work (Orion Communities (Lutfiyya, 1991) and Camp Hill Village, Kimberton Hills (Zipperlen & O'Brien, 1994)).

...A citizen advocacy project dedicated to forming and supporting relationships for socially excluded people.

...A project to assist people with disabilities to find affordable housing and share households with people who are not disabled.

...An alternative school.

...A medical practice where physicians and nurses focus their complementary skills on promoting wellness.

...Several connected efforts to reclaim public space including renovation of historic buildings, the development of a local cultural and craft center, and the creation of a common recreational space.

Though physically dispersed throughout the area and organizationally distinct, these efforts interpenetrate. One of the intentional communities farms bio-dynamically. Another biodynamic farm offers work to intentional community members with disabilities. Partners in the law practice are active in the reclamation of public space. Children from many of the households linked to the intentional communities go to the alternative school. A number of people from each effort attend the medical practice and share in the social and cultural activities sponsored by the alternative school and the intentional communities.

The context

Like many other desirable places to live within commuting distance of major cities, rapid growth shapes the area and threatens some of the qualities that make it a good place to move. Local community building efforts are increasingly influenced by...

...widening highways and more car traffic

...a growing proportion of people who leave the area for their work —often both members of couples who live together

...more houses built by large outside development companies rather than by the people who will live in them or by local housing developers

...more money spent in malls and chain restaurants than in downtown, local business

...more people who plan to live in the area for only a year or two and have chosen their location more because of house prices than because they want to settle down

...more people whose demands for city conveniences and opportunities in the country increases the rate of change in the economic and physical environment

...widespread concern about crime and security because there are more strangers and greater worry about strangers

...increasing housing costs, which more tightly squeeze poor people and people who work locally at relatively low paying jobs

...-greater conflict among people who do not know one another plus more pressure on local government to deal with complex issues, thus greater pressure toward formal regulation and formal systems and greater pressure to withdraw from local politics

...deep hunger among growing numbers of people for personal involvement, cultural expression, good food, healthy recreation, and meaning

The shifts expressed in these trends set the challenge for community builders: *What can we contribute that will develop the positive possibilities in this rapidly changing environment, where many changes could undermine our purposes?*

Most of the people involved in these community building efforts immigrated to the area —some from Europe, others from nearer by. They believe that community building proceeds from personal and organizational commitment to a particular place. Many have chosen —often at some risk— to be where they are, doing what they are doing. Many speak of the place and its people choosing them. Thus, they stand between people native to the area and people moving into new housing developments.

The creation of healthy community

Many of these community builders share a guiding metaphor that suggests how healthy community grows.

Just as healthy soil contains myriad species and substances including those associated with disease, and every human body provides a home to many microorganisms including those associated with sickness, so healthy community contains many potentials including those associated with oppression and neglect and abuse. In any of these living organisms, health results from knowledgeably balancing a wide field of sometimes opposing forces, but not from single minded attempts to destroy disease in individual segments.

Trying to maintain health just by identifying and eradicating all toxins brings ironic results: life cannot thrive under sterile conditions. Sterilized soil develops petrochemical fertilizer dependency. A sterilized gut can't digest real food. A risk free environment imprisons people and stifles and stunts their growth. To cultivate health, we have to create an environment in which potentially destructive forces are harmonized and limited by rhythmically calling balancing forces into play. Nurturing health calls for reaching out to include a wider environment more than for reaching into isolated individuals. The more damaged the environment we are part of, the longer we will need to understand it and to develop the art to build up its life sustaining diversity.

Trying to restore health simply by isolating and destroying particular symptoms multiplies the probability of new maladies: some development only comes by living with and through suffering. Poisoning the "bad" bugs enlarges the niche available to other crop destroyers. Knocking out every infection with antibiotics encourages the growth of more complex, better adapted bacteria. Blaming and ejecting one member as the cause of disharmony masks conflict in the community and sets the stage for the next episode of scapegoating.

To restore health we have to allow illness to express -and perhaps to mend- our imbalances. We can often soothe discomfort and frequently limit destruction without stamping out symptoms before we have read them as signs. Circumstances may lead us to reach for the pesticide or the antibiotic or the tranquillizer, but we will intervene mindful of the cascading effects of intervention and without the illusion that we are increasing health by decreasing disease.

Trying to understand health solely by expanding the catalog of specific causes of ever more precisely categorized diseases blinds one eye. Some illness may be adequately described by squinting down the barrel of a microscope, but health can only be understood in stereoscopic depth and through a broad scan. Laboratory intervention of ever stronger agents to search and destroy pests contributes nothing to observing, understanding and strengthening the ecological balance of a particular field. Assaying the agent of a symptom ignores the question of the meaning of this disease in this particular person's life. Analyzing negative incidents to lengthen the list of bad practices forbidden by regulation fails to raise consciousness of how the people in a particular household can live well together in the face of a specific difficulty.

To understand health we look at health. To see health we recognize ourselves as co-creators of health in a widening web of earthly, human, and spiritual relationships. To weave a stronger web of relationships, we increase individual and collective consciousness of the ties that include us and carry us through time by taking practical action based on the interdependencies we realize. To nurture consciousness, we open ourselves to recognize our diverse interdependencies and to request other's collaboration.

Cultivating health depends on acting together to overcome the fear that we struggle alone and futilely for survival against a hostile and meaningless environment. Empowered action follows a deepening understanding that we develop in what Scott Williamson, founder of London's Pioneer Health Centre called, "progressive mutual synthesis" with our environment: the growing health of each organism enriches the environment and the enriched environment increases the health of each organism within it. Knowledgeable action depends on learning to balance focused effort to impose order with effort to create conditions through which order will increase over time.

Some signs of community building

Despite their independent origin and their lack of coordination mechanisms (most people who gathered to share their experiences recognized one another, but this was the first time they had gathered to talk about their community building efforts and a number of people were introduced for the first time), these efforts seem connected by several common threads, which might be expressed this way.

- Through sustained work over years, efforts that build community touch fundamental, everyday concerns...

  ...to be healthy and to die well

  ...to join in making safe and welcoming homes in which each member of the household can discover and express individual gifts

  ...to support children's development and education in ways that allow the whole person to flower

  ...to have a safe place to be in times of confusion, crisis, or disruption

  ...to eat in a way that is healthy for the person and for the earth

  ...to have times and places for gathering to share, to learn, to celebrate, to express and to enjoy the beautiful, and to welcome strangers into public life

  ...to make agreements, resolve conflicts and ratify social arrangements in ways that respect relationships

  ...to reclaim and reanimate the land and soil and disused or misused buildings

  ...to learn how to do good work by developing skills and sharing knowledge through apprenticeship, by sharing with colleagues, and by experimenting to learn new ways to work, new ways to sustain economic support, and new ways to share the fruits of work

...to reach out to people in other places —with recognition that local efforts are local expressions of ideas catching fire in many places— to weave networks, to share information, and to share support

o Community builders encourage the life and development of community by working to

...shorten the distance between people's everyday life experience and the cycles of the living earth

...reclaim everyday patterns of work, rest, meals, and entertainment through thoughtful use of time

...increase the goods households and associations produce for themselves and decrease the amount of products individuals consume

...discover the possibilities that arise from the limits of a particular place and time by raising basic questions., such as: "What is the best use of this place now?" "What kind and what level of activity can this place sustain over time?" "What is the right use of our moral, economic, and cooperative power?"

...encouraging investment in the future and thinking of the effects that present actions beyond this lifetime

...heal the divisions among people on the basis of obvious difference by making room for excluded people in every place and activity

...encourage mutual help with each person contributing according to individual gift and ability

...search for ways to use property and money cooperatively which move beyond usual relationships of consumer/producer, or employer/employee, or professional/client

...encourage communal recognition of suffering and vulnerability, and thoughtful action to support one another rather than splitting care off from daily life and assigning responsibility to professional services

o Community builders transform themselves as they...

...invite others to create with them rather than simply being the objects of their good intentions or perplexed spectators

...open their own minds and hearts to discover allies by seeking common interests and ways to work with other people and groups, including those who may seem "unlikely" at first

...find energy for their work together without fighting enemies or putting down the unwashed

...seek wisdom to deal with the disappointments of broken promises, failed relationships, and failed projects

...appreciate the time development takes

...cultivate discernment and courage to deal with the dilemmas arising from tensions between: doing things right, according to shared and personal ideals, *and* doing it here with the resources available now; doing what can be done now *and* doing for all needs; celebrating what has been accomplished *and* recognizing shortcomings and failures

...create new social arrangements -such as support circles and citizen advocacy for excluded people- to fulfill what emerges as missing

...discover organizational and legal forms that better express their sense of the right relationship to property, employment, and profit such as land trusts, partnerships, and cooperatives

...awaken to the interconnections among various efforts to build community and look for ways to strengthen other efforts

...open to questions and challenges from one another and from outsiders

...seek the confidence to act in willingness to ask for and give support and assistance

Of course, none of these local manifestations are the signs of realized perfection. People committed to community building appear to be as fallible as any other group of people — though they seem to be less bothered about recognizing their fallibility than many other groups. These are the signs of people working hard to make their ideals real so that they may contribute to sustaining and building the earth and the intricate, fragile webs of relationships that all life on earth depends upon.

Citizen Advocacy

Conceptualized by Wolf Wolfensberger nearly 30 years ago, citizen advocacy is the preoccupation of a small, committed group of people who focus their talents on bringing vulnerable people together, one-to-one with citizens who are ready, willing, and able to protect them, to advocate for them, and often to form an important personal relationship with them.

Citizen Advocacy is a demanding social art. Those who practice it accept a discipline like that of a sonnet writer: clear definitions and principles for action shape their creative efforts. This chapter sketches these definitions and principles from the point of view of the experience of people in Georgia, who have had the opportunity to develop citizen advocacy programs over the past 20 years.*

A definition of citizen advocacy

A valued citizen who is unpaid and independent of human services creates a relationship with a person who is vulnerable and at risk of social exclusion and chooses one or several of many ways to understand, respond to, and represent that person's interests as if they were the advocate's own thus protecting their partner and bringing their partner's gifts and concerns into the circles of ordinary community life. A "valued citizen" is someone who is richly connected to the networks of people and associations that make up community life and willing and able to act with —and, if need be, on behalf of— another person. Citizen advocacy experience shows that people are rich in these valuable capacities regardless of social class, race, sex, and level of formal education.

Of course these vital relationships occur naturally and flourish without outside support. But the widespread practice of segregating people into professionally controlled settings on the basis of prejudices about disability greatly decreases the chances that

* For a somewhat different way to understand citizen advocacy, which is generally more consistent with the way Wolf Wolfensberger currently teaches about it, see the various issues of *The Citizen Advocacy Forum*.

people who are not disabled will know a person with a disability. Citizen advocacy programs are focused on arranging and supporting relationships among people who otherwise would not meet.

The importance of citizen advocacy

Good intentions and prejudice have combined to separate many people with disabilities into professionally controlled environments. Institutions, nursing homes, many board and care homes, and too many community residences, workshops, activity programs and special education programs segregate people —not for short periods of effective treatment but for years. Someone who is nothing but a client leads a constrained life, handicapped by being cut off from essential social and civic resources.

Relationships

There are a variety of different roles a citizen advocacy may adopt in order to understand and represent a vulnerable person's interests as if they were his or her own. A friend is someone to count on, someone to do and talk about things with, someone to share joys and sorrows and to exchange personal support. A mentor takes a personal interest in helping another person discover and develop skills and talents. An assistant chooses to help out with practical things. An ally stands with a person to help him or her get what is necessary for a decent life. A protector stands up for a person who is vulnerable to abuse or incompetent treatment. Those with very few good relationships will feel lonely and be vulnerable.

Writing in straight lines creates a trap because most actual relationships can't be neatly classified. Mentors can be friends. Friends can be protectors. Assistants can be mentors. The list is just a way to suggest that there are many ways to be in a relationship. A citizen advocacy program doesn't exist to choose among them but to begin and support a variety of different types of relationships.

Networks

Networks of people share some common interest and exchange information, access to other people, tools, favors, influence, and assistance. People enlist others to join their cause, solicit donations, get advice about the best doctor, discover new trends, locate a place to buy at a discount, borrow a router, and find job leads and business prospects from among their network of contacts. Those without networks of contacts are likely to be ill informed, and ineffective since they must do things in the least efficient, most expensive way.

Memberships

Membership in formal and informal associations – neighborhood associations, political clubs, churches and church groups, civic organizations, softball teams, and the people who hang around together at the gas station- offers group support for one's interests, status, and the possibility of civic and political influence. Those with no memberships are likely to be isolated and powerless and to seem a stranger to others.

Positive roles

Because of the way services are designed many people with disabilities are reduced to commodities: they are valuable because other people have jobs housing them and looking after them. Few people who rely very much on services have these everyday roles available to them: renter, home owner, worker, business person, investor, volunteer doing useful work, or student preparing for a "real job." Most Americans who rely services are cash and asset poor by public policy: publicly funded services are usually arranged to make people with assets ineligible, to pauperize people who enter services with assets, to discourage people from earning, and to offer people a level of cash payment well below a living wage. Those without positive roles in the local economy are likely to have little money, limited security in housing, few opportunities to contribute, and diminished standing in negotiating conflicts because of the prejudices summed up in the phrase "beggars can't be choosers".

Citizen advocacy responds to people's exclusion by making and supporting personal relationships between people with very few resources and people with many resources which have their roots outside the human service system. Citizen advocates can contribute in a variety of ways: they offer the benefits of personal relationship, provide introductions to new people, help a person make contacts or use their network of contacts on the person's behalf, enlist the support of community associations, and sponsor a person's membership in community associations. They can build a variety of bridges.

Citizen advocacy strengthens community

Exclusion of people with disabilities diminishes community in at least four ways: local people, associations, and enterprises are deprived of the energy, skills, knowledge and other gifts that a person with a disability can bring; the help that a person with a disability may need can become excessively costly as the human service system implements "all or nothing" service arrangements instead of applying its resources to support the people who care for and include a person; many ordinary people don't develop or use their competencies for caring and conclude that only professionals know how to care; and people separate from one another to hide the human realities of imperfection, dependency, fallibility, and suffering rather than gathering together to learn their lessons. Citizen advocacy encourages others to welcome people with disabilities as friends, neighbors, and fellow citizens who may need extra help or accommodation. It appeals to people's neighborliness, common sense, everyday skills, and human courage rather than to professionalized solutions. It is one way to build community competence.

Many people with disabilities are handicapped by rejection and unfair treatment which is justified by prejudiced beliefs. Prejudices remain undisturbed as long as people remain apart. Citizen advocacy is one way to bring people together and dissolve prejudices.

Many people with disabilities rely on human services that deal with them as one of a group and these services make few allowances for individual differences unless a person has an ally. Human services often have confusing requirements and procedures and sometimes withhold important information; an outsiders eye and voice can make an important difference to the quality of service a marginalized person receives. Some human services are neglectful and some abuse people; though independent people with no special authority can seldom reform such settings they can sometimes make official systems for protecting people work better, and some advocates have simply taken people away from abusive places. Citizen advocacy is one way to make services do better what they are able to do.

A growing number of people believe that people with disabilities are at risk of a powerful, and largely hidden social process Wolf Wolfensberger has named deathmaking. Under these conditions only strong personal commitments by courageous people can hope to protect vulnerable individuals. Citizen advocacy is one way to form such commitments.

There are many ways to encourage caring and civic responsibility, to bring people with disabilities together with other citizens, and to protect and promote the interests of people with disabilities. Each way can make a real contribution; each has limitations. Citizen advocacy is one clear, direct approach: the formation and support of responsible personal relationships. Its worth does not depend on being the best solution for everyone or on beating out other approaches but on its distinctive contribution to community life.

How a successful citizen advocacy program develops

A successful citizen advocacy program is animated by a core group, who commit themselves to learning through public action how to implement citizen advocacy in their community. This core group of committed people must include both community members and program staff. The work of a citizen advocacy coordinator, as key staff are known, can't be organized and supervised in the typical pattern of impersonal board-staff relationships because it requires too much commitment to principled action. Typically, some core group members will function as the program's board (though not every board member may be a core group member), others will work as staff, others may be key advisers. Core group members may shift among roles. The core group is defined by shared values and continuity over time

Committed people involve themselves in learning, over time, how to do four closely related tasks with increasing effectiveness and efficiency.

Achieve and maintain focus

Focus grows as people develop and deepen their own understanding and personal commitment to citizen advocacy through reflection on the situation of people with disabilities and the importance of unpaid personal relationships in many people's lives, consideration of the capacities their fellow citizens and their community associations, and study of citizen advocacy principles and practice.

Having attained focus, core group members assess each decision they make in terms of their shared principles; communicate their understanding to others in a way that inspires committed action; make time to share ideas and exchange resources with core groups who are implementing citizen advocacy in other places; and, rigorously evaluate their program's performance —periodically with the help of an outside team experienced in citizen advocacy— celebrating successes and supporting one another to learn from shortcomings and failures.

Make and support relationships

The mission of the citizen advocacy program is to make and support a growing number and variety of citizen advocacy relationships by insuring that those who work as citizen advocacy coordinators have opportunities to understand citizen advocacy and to clarify its relationship to their personal values and sense of mission; get opportunities to learn how to do a coordinator's work, at least by a brief apprenticeship with an experienced coordinator; experience adequate, if modest, income, benefits, and working conditions; get regular help in remembering the meaning in the routine of daily work, in failures and in successes; find practical ways to manage their time and balance their efforts among the key citizen advocacy activities; implement plans for maintaining a diversity and variety of relationships; and get assistance in problem solving and practical help making the contacts necessary to learn about their community, to recruit people with disabilities, and to recruit citizen advocates.

Develop roots in their community

Community roots give the program long term access to the resources it needs: people who will enter and support relationships; people who will invite others into relationships; the independence to support a variety of citizen actions, and the funds necessary to operate the program over time. This means sharing and increasing knowledge of the local community, especially its associational life; defining a clear identity for the program; taking a clear position distinct from human services by making alliances with associations involved in community regeneration rather than joining up with the human service system; and drawing on a variety of funding sources and steadily increasing the proportion of funding from sources outside the human service system.

Create an effective organization

Formal and informal structures are necessary to support ongoing action. The core group needs well defined ways to receive and effectively manage funds; employ staff; make decisions consistent with citizen advocacy focus; provide mutual support and problem solving; expand its membership in a way that increases the depth of its roots throughout the community and provide broad support for the program and the people who work as citizen advocacy coordinators; and dissolve the program if it becomes impossible to implement citizen advocacy.

Founding principles

A citizen advocacy program is based on principles which test each of the many decisions that shape the program, from where to locate and how to seek funds to how coordinators manage their daily schedule. These principles define what a citizen advocacy program is and what direction is important to maintain over time. Once there is agreement about what citizen advocacy is, there is room for much creativity in how to do it in a particular time and place.

Relationship focus

The focus of all of the energy available for the program is on creating and supporting a variety of responsible personal relationships that encourage identification with and active protection and representation of the interests of the person with a disability, bring the person with a disability into social and community life, and usually involve long term commitments.

This means that the citizen advocacy program does not do other worthy things that would detract from this focus. Citizen advocacy program staff do not themselves do individual or social advocacy as part of their jobs. The citizen advocacy program itself does not get involved with broader issues concerning people with disabilities —such as lobbying, public education or participating as an office in local service planning or governance— though people in citizen advocacy relationships are encouraged to do so. The citizen advocacy program itself does not set up, sponsor or staff self-advocacy or family advocacy groups, though people in citizen advocacy relationships may choose to do so.

Diverse relationships

The citizen advocacy program purposely seeks diversity among the people it invites into relationships. Over time, the program will planfully involve people from many parts of the community and reach out to people with disabilities of different ages; of different abilities, including people with profound disabilities and people who do not apparently have the ability to respond to other people; and in different living situations, including people who live on their own, people who live with their families, people who live in residential programs, and people in public and private institutions.

Over time, people will be involved in relationships that can be described in a variety of different ways. If an outsider found out what was happening in all of the relationships at a point in time, they would identify many different things going on in the relationships.

- Some people simply share time and activities;
- Some people are allies, actively working to pursue a goal of importance to the person with a disability, such as getting a job or a home or getting better service from an agency;
- Some people help the person with a disability to define and develop gifts and interests, perhaps by sharing a skill;
- Some people protect a person who is vulnerable to abuse or neglect, perhaps by monitoring a potentially dangerous situation, perhaps by speaking up for the person to responsible authorities, perhaps by arranging or providing a safe alternative;
- Some people help with everyday or occasional decisions or tasks; and sometimes these relationships will have been formalized by an outside authority as when a person acts as a guardian of property or person, a surrogate parent, or as a payee and manager of the person's pension or benefits;
- Some people offer a home and a share in their family life; sometimes this will be formalized by adoption;
- A growing number of relationships will have lasted a long time though some will be arranged for a specific, short term purpose;
- There will be surprises; people in relationships will create new possibilities.

Freedom of relationship

Citizen advocates freely choose to enter a relationship which is independent of the human service system and not controlled by the citizen advocacy program. Citizen advocacy relationships are voluntary, but citizen advocates are not "volunteers" to an agency: they find direction in their relationship; not from an outside supervisor.

As much as possible, people with disabilities should choose

relationships as well. But the citizen advocacy program may match citizen advocates with people who cannot chose or even with people who reject a personal relationship. Some people with disabilities may be in circumstances that make it difficult to determine choice: some people cannot speak, some people have such limited experiences as to make informed consent difficult, others are in settings that exercise so much control over daily life as to make choice itself a problem, and some people's disability makes relationships difficult. A program may recruit an advocate whose first task is to discover how to understand and represent the interests of a person at great risk at least in part because he or she cannot or will not relate to the advocate.

Freedom for action

Citizen advocates are independent of human services.

The citizen advocacy program encourages the citizen advocate to identify with the person with a disability and look at situations from his or her point of view. The program supports the citizen advocate in recognizing and acting on negative, unhelpful, or conflicting human service perspectives;

The citizen advocacy program recruits people with disabilities and supports relationships in ways that protect advocate independence;

The citizen advocacy program encourages the citizen advocate to look outside the human service system for resources and solutions. The office seeks, celebrates, and shares examples of civic or personal responsibility.

Citizen advocates are supported by the citizen advocacy program but not supervised, evaluated, or fired by the citizen advocacy program. They are not paid or compensated in any way by or because of the program.

A positive example

The citizen advocacy program itself is a model of positive interactions and interpretations of people with disabilities.

Interested people with disabilities are members of the core group and the formal board.

The program seeks an accurate, positive image for people with disabilities in its deliberations, literature, its own fund raising methods and those of program donors, office location, design, and decor. Stigmatizing language and images are identified and avoided.

Core group members are respectful of the people they meet as representatives of the citizen advocacy program.

Community roots

The program defines its identity and develops its support in the community, is able to act independently of the human service system, and is not identified with the human service system. The human service system is the collection of managed, professionally staffed agencies organized to serve people who are eligible by reason of disability or some other perceived deficit along with the agencies that coordinate and raise funds for them. The human service system is mostly funded by government, sometimes with participation from charities whose aim is to assist an eligible class of people. Government may operate parts of the human service system directly, but in most communities a mix of government, voluntary non-profit, and proprietary for profit agents comprise the system. The human service system combines efforts to change eligible people, efforts to provide income supports in cash or in kind, efforts to provide personal assistance such as attendant care, and efforts to control eligible people. Users of the system very rarely have control of the services they receive; they are seldom, for example, purchasers of the services they choose, and professionals in the system usually feel they know best. In many communities, there is a stigma attached simply to being a client of the human service system. The human service system can be helpful to people with disabilities but —unless it is exceptionally well led and carefully safeguarded— it is likely to isolate its users from contact with ordinary people and valued community places, to fail to take adequate account of its users individuality, and even to expose its users to neglect and abuse. Citizen advocacy is distinct from the human service system in that it strives to initiate and support freely given relationships, it does not assess and prescribe for people, it does not assume the superiority of professional solutions over personal judgements, and it does not aspire to define and serve all of the members of an eligible class. The fact that citizen advocacy maintains a distinction from the human service system is not in itself a virtue. It simply defines a place to begin work.

The program is not administered by a service providing agency. The citizen advocacy office is not located with or within a human service providing agency;

The program is funded in a way that offers the possibility of independent action and does not impose tasks, deadlines, or accountability measures that make it impossible to develop and run a citizen advocacy program.

People who work as citizen advocacy coordinators do not identify themselves as or with human service workers; their primary alliances are with people and groups who are working to regenerate community;

The core group grows to include people with a variety of perspectives and connections to local people and financial resources; sometimes the only thing core group members will agree upon is the importance of citizen advocacy;

The core group works systematically to increase the proportion of funding from sources that are not usually associated with the human services. They seek funds that will position them among the local associations that are committed to regenerating community.

Afterword

Concluding Thoughts

Judith Snow

As I read John O'Brien and Connie Llyle O'Brien's words I often had tears running down my face. This is a very important book.

Members of each other. What a simple phrase to embrace the image of a world where belonging is open to everyone! What longing for fulfillment those words evoke in me!

Rejection is daily bread for people who are called disabled and their friends. How graphically John and Connie's words and stories describe the isolation, the confusion and especially the blindness to all that might be possible if only we were open to each other's presence!

What joy to read words and stories of the power in welcoming each other into relationship - through entering associations, building partnerships through Citizen Advocacy, through invitation and action in circles. Of course sometimes mutual membership is discovered by chance simply because we are human and have the capacity to encounter each other.

It is said that Moses sinned and so God would not let him enter the Promised Land. Instead God gave Moses a great vision of the wonderful society that the Israelites would create in the future.

I think I have a sense of the bitter sweet vision that Moses must have experienced. He came so close and yet was denied. Clearly it is in our human grasp to see each other differently, to change our structures so that the barriers are leveled and to embrace each other's presence as full members of human society. We have created many examples already that show us what a benefit being members of each other would be to ourselves and to our communities.

Yet most of us are denied the fulfillment of this knowledge and experience. Instead of embracing solidarity most of us live within the boundaries created by prejudice and structures that divide.

This book must finish with a challenge to each of us. We must overcome resignation and create. Our new sculpture must be a unique one - formed in response to the vision that the words "members of each other" call forth. It must be a work of human relationship. We have seen the examples; we have been shown the path.

We can become members of each other only by being members of each other. May these words and stories inspire us along the way.

Judith A. Snow

Judith Snow is an advocate, philosopher, writer, speaker and student of life. She is a founding member of the Centre for Integrated Education and Community. She lives and works and travels from Toronto..

Resources

For more information about citizen advocacy, contact:

Georgia Advocacy Office
999 Peachtree St. NE, Suite 890
Atlanta, GA 30309

The Citizen Advocacy Forum
PO Box 86
Beaver, PA 15009

For more information about assisting people to become members of community associations, contact:

Kathy Bartholomew-Lorimer
1929 West Schiller
Chicago, IL 60622

Association Integration Project
56 Suffolk St., Suite 500
Holyoke, MA 01040

For more information about circles of support, contact:

Centre for Integrated Education and Community
24 Thome Crescent
Toronto, ON M6H 2S5

Communitas
P.O. Box 374
Manchester, CT 06040

References

Adler, D. (1993). Perspectives of a support worker. In Racino, J, Walker, P., O'Connor, S, and Taylor, S., Eds. *Housing, support, and community: Choices and strategies for adults with disabilities.* Baltimore: Paul Brookes Publishing. Pp. 217-231.

Ailred of Rievaulx (1942). *Christian friendship.* (H. Talbot, Trans.). London: The Catholic Book Club.

Anderson, J., Lakin, KC, Hill, BK, & Chen, T. (1992). Social Integration of older persons with mental retardation in residential facilities. *American Journal on Mental Retardation,* 96 (5), 488-501.

Aristotle (1955). *The ethics of Aristotle: The Nicomachean ethics, Books 8-9.* (J. Thomson & H. Tredennick, Trans.) London: Penguin Books.

Atkinson, D. (1986). Engaging competent others: A study of the support networks of people with mental handicap. Br*itish Journal of Social Work, 16, Supplement,* 83-101.

Atkinson, D. & Williams, F., (Eds.) (1990). *Know me as I am: An anthology of prose, poetry and art by people with learning difficulties.* London: Hodder & Stoughton.

Barnes, C. (1990). *'Cabbage syndrome': The social construction of dependence.* London: Falmer.

Bateson. M.C. (1988). *Composing a life.* NY: Atlantic Monthly Press.

Baxter, A. (1991). *How citizen advocacy coordinators do their work.* Atlanta, GA: Georgia Advocacy Office.

Beeman, P., Ducharme, G., & Mount, B. (1989). *One candle power: Building bridges into community life with people with disabilities.* Manchester, CT: Communitas.

Bellah, R., Madsen, R., Sullivan, W., Swidler, A. & Tipton, S. (1985). *Habits of the heart: Individualism and commitment in American life.* Berkeley, CA: University of California Press.

Berry, W. (1986). *The wild birds: Six stories of the Port William membership.* San Francisco: North Point Press.

Bevilacqua, C. (May, 1992). Poetry by students using facilitated communication. *TASH Newsletter, 16,* 5, p. 6.

Berkson, G. & Romer, D. (1981). A letter to a developmental disabilities administrator. In R. Bruininks, C. E. Meyers, B. Sigford, & K.C. Lakin, (Eds.) Deinstitutionalization *and community adjustment of mentally retarded people.* AAMR Monograph Number 4. Washington, DC: AAMR.

Benviniste, E. (1973). *Indo-European Language and Society.* Coral Gabels, FL: University of Florida Press.

Biklen, D. (1992). *Schooling without labels: Parents, educators, and inclusive education.* Philadelphia, PA: Temple University Press.

Bogdan, R. & Taylor, S. (1987). Toward a sociology of acceptance: The other side of the study of deviance. *Social Policy, 18,* 34-39.

Bogdan, R. & Taylor, S. (1989). Relationships with severely disabled people: The social construction of humanness. *Social Problems, 36* (2), 135-148.

Bogdan, R. (1987). We *take care of our own: Georgia Citizen Advocacy in Savannah and Macon.* Syracuse, NY: Center on Human Policy.

Booth, W. (1988). *The company we keep: An ethics of fiction.* Berkeley, CA: University of California Press.

Buber, M. quoted in Friedman, M.S. (1960). *Martin Buber: The life of dialogue.* Harper Torchbooks, New York, p. 81.

Bulmer, M. (1987). *The social basis of community care.* London: Allen & Unwin.

Coyne, J., Wortman, C., & Lehman, D. The other side of support: Emotional overinvolvement and miscarried helping. In B. Gottlieb (Ed.), *Marshaling social support: Formats, processes, and effects* (pp. 11-51). Newbury Park, CA: Sage Publications.

Crossley, R. & McDonald, A. (1984). *Annie's coming out (revised edition).* Ringwood, Victoria: Penguin Books Australia.

Easterling, P. (1989). Friendship and the Greeks. In R. Porter & S. Tomaselli (Eds.), *The dialectics of friendship.* New York: Routledge.

Edgerton, R. (1988). Aging in the community: A matter of choice. *American Journal on Mental Retardation, 92,* 4, 331-335.

Edgerton, R. (1991). Conclusion. In R. Edgerton & M. Gaston, (Eds.) "I've seen it all!" Lives of older persons with mental retardation in the community. Baltimore, MD: Paul Brookes Publishing Co.

Edwards, J. & Dawson, D. (1983). *My friend David: A source book about Down's syndrome and a personal story about friendship.* Portland, OR: Ednick.

Elks, M. (1990). Lessons from Annie's Coming Out. *National Council on Intellectual Disability: Interaction 4,* 1, 7-17.

Evans, D. (1983). *The lives of mentally retarded people.* Boulder, CO: Westview.

Evans, G. & Murcott, A. (1990) Community care: Relationships and control. *Disability, Handicap & Society, 5,* 2, 123-135.

Ferguson, P., Hibbard, M., Leinen, J. & Schaff, S. (1990). Supported community life: Disability policy and the renewal of mediating structures. *Journal of Disability Policy Studies, 1,* 1: 10-35.

Finch, J. (1989). Social policy, social engineering, and the family in the 1990s. In M. Bulmer, J. Lewis, & D. Piachaud (Eds.), *The goals of social policy.* London: Unwin Hyman.

Firth, H. & Rapley, M. (1990). *From acquaintance to friendship: Issues for people with learning disabilities.* Kidderminster, Worcs.: British Institute of Mental Handicap Publications.

Flynn, M. (1989). *Independent living for adults with mental handicap: A place of my own.* London: Cassell Educational Ltd.

Flynn, M. (1991). *Moving On 2: Report from a conference of service users exploring friendship.* London: National Development Team for People with Learning Difficulties.

Gallagher, H. (1989). Evolving medical attitudes toward the quality of life. In B. Duncan & D. Woods (Eds.), *Ethical issues in disability and rehabilitation* (pp. 17-25). New York: World Rehabilitation Fund.

Gilligan, C. (1982). *In a different voice: Psychological theory and women's development.* Cambridge, MA: Harvard University Press.

Glouberman, S. (1990). *Keepers: Inside stories from total institutions.* London: King Edward's Hospital Fund for London.

Gottlieb, B. (1988), Marshaling social support: The state of the art in research and practice. In B. Gottlieb (Ed.), *Marshaling social support: Formats, processes, and effects,* pp. 11-51. Newbury Park, CA: Sage Publications.

Gretz, S. (1991). Citizen participation: Connecting people to associational life. In D. Schwartz, *The other side of the river: The conceptual/social revolution in developmental disabilities.* Cambridge, MA: Brookline.

Gretz, S. (1988, September). About being a citizen. *The Developmental Disabilities Planner, 5,* 2, p 1, 4.

Hagner, D. (1989). *The social integration of supported employees: A qualitative study.* Syracuse, NY: Center on Human Policy

Heilbrun, C. (1988). Writing *a woman's life.* New York: W.W. Norton.

Heumann, J. (1993). A disabled woman's reflections: Myths and realities of integration. In J. Racino, P. Walker, S. O'Connor, & S. Taylor, (Eds.) *Housing, support, and community: Choices and strategies for adults with disabilities.* Baltimore, MD: Paul Brookes Publishing Co.

Hildebrand, A. (1991). Asking for citizen advocates in Beaver County. In D. Schwartz, *The other side of the river: The conceptual/social revolution in developmental disabilities.* Cambridge, MA: Brookline.

Hill, B., Rotegard, L., & Bruininks, R. Quality of life of mentally retarded people in residential care. *Social Work,* 29, 275-281.

House, J., Umberson, D. & Landis, K. (1988). Structures and processes of social support, *Annual Review of Sociology,* 14: 293-318.

Hunt, M.E. (1991). *Fierce tenderness: A feminist theology of friendship.* New York: Crossroad.

Illich, I. (1976). *Medical nemesis: The expropriation of health.* NY: Pantheon.

Joyce, S. (Ed.). *Collages: Sketches of a support circle.* Realizations, PO Box 1430, Station B, London, Ontario N6A 5M2.

Kallenback, D. & Lyons, A. (1989). *Government spending for the poor in Cook County, Illinois: Can we do better?* Evanston, IL: Center for Urban Affairs and Policy research, Northwestern University.

Kegan, R. (1982). *The evolving self: Problem and process in human development.* Cambridge, MA: Harvard University Press.

Kretzmann, J. and McKnight, J. (1993). *Building community from the inside out: A path toward finding and mobilizing a community's assets.* Center for Urban Affairs and Policy Research, Northwestern University, 2040 Sheridan Rd, Evanston, IL 60208.

LaFrancis, M. (1990). *Welcoming newcomers to community groups.* Holyoke, MA: Education for Community Initiatives.

Landesman-Dwyer, S., Berkson, G., & Romer, D. (1979). Affiliation and friendship of mentally retarded residents in group homes. *American Journal of Mental Deficiency, 83,* 6, 571-580.

Lasch, C. (1978). *The culture of narcissism.* New York: Norton.

Leatham, G. & Duck, S, (1990). Conversations with friends and the dynamics of social support. In S. Duck (Ed.) *Personal relationships and social support* (pp. 1-29). Newbury Park, CA: Sage Publications.

LeWare, M. (1989). Community opens it's church doors for Betty. Building bridges: Stories about community building in Logan Square. 1: 1, pp. 1-2.

Lewin, T. (1990, 28 October). When the retarded grow old: A special report. *The New York Times,* pp. 1, 13.

Lord, J. & Pedlar, A. (1990). *Life in the community: Four years after the close of an institution.* Kitchner, ON: Centre for Research & Education in Human Services.

Ludlum, C. (1991). The power of a circle of support. In B. Mount, *Dare to dream: An analysis of the conditions leading to personal change for people with disabilities.* Manchester, CT: Communitas.

Ludlum, C. (1988). My circle. In B. Mount, P. Beeman, & G. Ducharme, *What are we learning about circles of support?* Manchester, CT: Communitas.

Lutfiyya, Z. (1991). Mighty prophets of the future: The Orion Community. In, S. Taylor, R. Bogdan,, & J. Racino (Eds.) *Life in the community: Case studies of organizations supporting people with disabilities.* Baltimore, MD: Paul Brookes Publishers, p. 227-241.

Lutfiyya, Z. (1990). *Affectionate bonds: What we can learn by listening to friends.* -Syracuse, NY: Center on Human Policy.

Lutfiyya, Z. (1989). *The phenomenology of relationships between typical and disabled people.* Doctoral dissertation, Syracuse University, Syracuse, NY.

MacAndrew, C. & Edgerton, R. (1966). On the possibility of friendship. *American Journal of Mental Deficiency, 70,* 612-621.

McFague, S. (1987). *Models of God: Theology for an ecological, nuclear age.* Philadelphia: Fortress Press.

McKnight, J. (1989a). *Beyond community services.* Center for Urban Affairs Paper. Evanston, IL: Northwestern University.

McKnight, J. (1989b). *First do no harm.* Center for Urban Affairs Paper. Evanston, IL: Northwestern University.

McKnight, J. (1987). Regenerating community. *Social Policy,* 17, (3), 54-58.

Martinez, C. (1988, April). Quality of life. Presentation to the US Commission on Civil Rights Conference on Quality of Life. Washington, DC.

Meadows, L. (1991), Kevin's story: Focus on capacity. In B. Mount, *Dare to dream: An analysis of the conditions leading to personal change for people with disabilities.* Manchester, CT: Communitas.

Melberg-Schwier, K. (1990). *Speakeasy: People with mental handicaps talk about their lives in institutions and in the community.* Austin, TX: Pro-Ed.

Mount, B. (1991). *Dare to dream: An analysis of the conditions leading to personal change for people with disabilities.* Communitas Publications, PO Box 374, Manchester CT, 06040.

O'Brien, J. (1988). Field notes from the Connecticut DMR Family Support Program evaluation.

O'Connell, M. (1990). *Community building in Logan Square: How a community grew stronger with the contributions of people with disabilities.* Evanston, IL: Northwestern University Center for Urban Affairs & Policy Research.

Opotow, S. (1990). Moral exclusion and injustice [Special issue]. *Journal of Social Issues, 46,* 1.

Ordinary Life Group (1988). *Ties and connections: An ordinary community life for people with learning difficulties.* London: Kings Fund Centre.

Oswin, M. (1991). *Am I allowed to cry? A study of bereavement amongst people who have learning difficulties.* London: Souvenir Press (Educational & Academic).

Osburn, J. (1988). *Welcome to the club: Report of an external evaluation of the Association Integration Project.* Holyoke, MA: Education for Community Initiatives.

Partridge, E. (1983). *A short etymological dictionary of modern English.* New York, NY: Crown Publishers.

Pealer, J. & O'Brien, J. (1985). *Personal relationships for people with developmental disabilities.* Proceedings of a Conference on Informal Support. Columbus, OH: Ohio Society for Autistic Citizens.

Pearpoint, J. (1990). *From behind the piano: The building of Judith Snow's unique circle of friends.* Toronto: Inclusion Press.

Perske, R. (1988). *Circles of friends: People with disabilities and their friends enrich the lives of one another.* Nashville, TN: Abingdon Press.

Piliavin, J. & Charng, H. (1990). Altruism: A review of recent theory and research. *Annual Review of Sociology,* 16: 27-65.

Pilisuk, M. & Parks, S. (1986). T*he healing web: Social networks and human survival.* Hanover, NH: University Press of New England.

Plato (1979). The *Lysis*. In D. Bolotin, *Plato's dialogue on friendship: An interpretation of the Lysis with a new translation*. Ithaca, NY: Cornell University Press.

Raymond, J. (1986). *A passion for friends: Toward a philosophy of female affection*. Boston: Beacon Press.

Richardson, A. & Ritchie, J. (1989) *Developing friendships: Enabling people with learning difficulties to make and maintain friends*. London: Policy Studies Institute.

Rudofsky, B. (1964). *Architecture without architects: A short introduction to non-pedigreed architecture*. Doubleday, Garden City, NY.

Sarason, S. (1988). *The Making of an American psychologist: An autobiography*. San Francisco: Jossey Bass.

Sarason, S., Carrol, C., Maton, K., Choen, S., & Lorentz, E. (1977). *Human services and resource networks*. San Francisco: Jossey Bass.

Schaefer, N. (1982). *Does she know she's there?* (updated edition). Toronto: Fitzhenry & Whiteside.

Shipley, J. (1984). *The origins of English words: A discursive dictionary of Indo-European roots*. Baltimore, MD: Johns Hopkins Press.

Shkilnyk, A. (1985). *A poison stronger than love: The destruction of an Ojibwa community*. New Haven: Yale University Press.

Snow, J. (1994). *What's really worth doing and how to do it: A book for people who love someone labeled disabled (possibly yourself)*. Toronto, ON: Inclusion Press.

Snow, J. (1991). *Dreaming, speaking, and creating: What I know about community*. Toronto: Centre for Integrated Education and Community.

Snow, J. (1990, September) *The meaning of support as I experience it*. Presentation to Policy Institute on Natural Support sponsored by The Center on Human Policy at Syracuse University, Syracuse, NY.

Snow, J. (1990) Bradwin Address to the 89th Annual Meeting of Frontier College. Reprinted in Pearpoint, J. *From behind the piano: The building of Judith Snow's unique circle of friends*. Inclusion Press, Toronto. Pp. 121-129.

Snow, J. (1989). Systems of support, A new vision. In S. Stainback, W. Stainback, & M. Forest (Eds.), *Educating all students in the mainstream of regular education*. Baltimore: Paul Brookes.

Snow, J. & Forest, M. (1988). *Support circles: Building a vision*. Toronto: Centre for Integrated Education and Community.

Strully, J. & Strully, C. Friendship and our children. *JASH, 10*, 4, 224-227.

Strully, J. & Strully, C. (1989). Friendships as an educational goal. In W. Stainback, S. Stainback. & M. Forest (Eds.), *Integrating regular and special education students*. Baltimore, MD: Paul Brookes Publishing Co.

Strully, J. & Strully, C. (1993). That which binds us: Friendships as a safe harbor in a storm. In A. Novak Amado, Ed., *Friends: Connections between persons with and without disabilities.* Baltimore, MD: Paul Brookes Publishing Co.

Taylor, C. (1991). *The malaise of modernity.* (CBC Massey lecture series, 1991). Concord, ON: Anansi Press.

Taylor, S., Bogdan, R., & Lutfiyya, Z. (1995). *The variety of community experience: qualitative studies of family and community life.* Baltimore, MD: Paul Brookes Publishing Co.

Taylor, S. & Bogdan, R. (1989). On accepting relationships between people with mental retardation and non-disabled people: Towards and understanding of acceptance. *Disability, Handicap & Society,* 4, 1, 21-36.

de Tocqueville, A. (1990). *Democracy in America (12th ed.)* [P. Bradley, Trans.], New York: Vintage Classics. [Original work published in 1848].

Traustadottir, R. (1990, March), Women, disability, and caring. *TASH Newsletter,* pp. 6-7.

Traustadottir, R. (1992). The gendered context of friendships. In A. Novak Amado, editor. *Friends: Connections between persons with and without disabilities.* Baltimore, MD: Paul Brookes Publishing Co.

Ungerson, C. (1987). *Policy is personal: Sex, gender, and informal care.* London: Tavistock Publications.

Vanier, J. (1992). *From Brokenness to Community.* The Wit Lectures, Harvard Divinity School. New York: Paulist Press.

Weiss, R. (1973). *Loneliness: The experience of emotional and social isolation.* Cambridge, MA: MIT Press.

Weiss, R. (1982). Loneliness: What we know about it and what we might do about it. In L. Peplow & S. Goldstein (Eds.), *Preventing the harmful consequences of severe and persistent loneliness.* Rockville, MD: NIMH.

Walker, A. (1986). Community care: Fact and fiction. In P. Wilmott, Ed. *The debate about community.* PSI Discussion paper No. 13. London: Policy Studies Institute.

Walker, A. (1982). *Community Care.* Oxford: Basil Blackwell.

Welch, S. (1990). *A feminist ethic of risk.* Minneapolis, MN: Augsberg Fortress Press.

Welty, E. & Sharp, R. (1991). *The Norton book of friendship.* New York: W.W. Norton.

Willmott, P. (1987). *Friendship networks and social support.* PSI Research Report No. 666. London: Policy Studies Institute.

Willmott, P. (1986). *Social networks, informal care, and public policy.* PSI Research Report No. 655. London: Policy Studies Institute.

Williams, P. (1977). *Our mutual handicap.* London: Campaign for the Mentally Handicapped.

Williams, R. (1989). *In a struggling voice.* Seattle, WA: TASH.

Wolfensberger, W. (1975). *The origin and nature of our institutional models.* Syracuse, NY: Human Policy Press.

Wolfensberger, W. (1991). *A brief introduction to social role valorization as a high-order concept for structuring human services.* Syracuse, NY: Training Institute for Human Service Planning (Syracuse University).

World Institute on Disability & Rutgers University Bureau of Economic Research (n.d.). *The Need for Personal Assistance.* Oakland, CA: World Institute on Disability.

Worth, P. (1990, July). Presentation to The Summer Institute on Inclusive Education, McGill University Faculty of Education, Montreal, PQ.

Zipperlen, H. & O'Brien, J. (1994). *Cultivating thinking hearts: Letters from the lifesharing safeguards project.* Harrisburg, PA: Developmental Disabilities Planning Council.

INCLUSION PRESS International

24 Thome Cresc.
Toronto, Ont. M6H 2S5
tel: 416-658-5363 fax: 416-658-5067
e-mail: 74640.1124@compuserve.com
Publishers: Jack Pearpoint & Marsha Forest

December, 1996 edition

Inclusion Press is a small independent press striving to produce readable, accessible, user-friendly books and resources about full inclusion in school, work, and community.

Our books are excellent resources for courses and conferences. Write/call for information re bulk rates for schools and voluntary/advocacy organizations. Inclusion Press can recommend packets of materials for your conferences, workshops, staff-development seminars and events.

Visit our WEB PAGE: http://inclusion.com

New Books! New Videos!

New MAPS Training Video

NEW

SHAFIK"S MAP

Prod: Inclusion Press & Parashoot

MAPS- step by step - John O'Brien facilitating Shafik Abu-Tahir's Map. How to make families partners in planning. Holistic, creative, colorful futures planning for people, families, organizations. + Judith Snow on Dreaming. (45 min)

PATH Training Video

NEW

Introduction to Path

Prod: Inclusion Press & Parashoot (35 min)

Exciting, creative, colorful futures planning tool. Jack & Marsha demonstrate 8 steps with an individual and his family. An excellent introduction - linked to the PATH book.

Friendship: It's About Time

NEW

Produced by Vision TV, Exec. Prod: Rita Deverell, Prod: Sadia Zaman

A 27 minute video exploration of friendship: joys, heartaches and maintenance, featuring Marsha, Jack and Judith.

Members of Each Other

Building Community in Company With People With Developmental Disabilities

NEW NEW

John O'Brien & Connie Lyle O'Brien

Remarkable & thought provoking - about building community.

What's Really Worth Doing

& How To DO IT! *by Judith Snow*

A book for people who love someone labeled disabled - possibly yourself. "This is a book of wisdom – and invitation to the dance of life." John McKnight

The Inclusion Papers

Strategies to Make Inclusion Happen

Jack Pearpoint & Marsha Forest

Practical, down to earth and sensible. Perfect for conferences, courses and workshops. Circles of Friends, MAPS, articles about drop-outs, kids at risk, Medical School course and more... graphics, poetry, overheads...

Classic Videos

Kids Belong Together

Prod: People First Assoc of Lethbridge, Alta Featuring the late Fr. Patrick Mackan – a celebration of friendship – MAPS in action.

With a Little Help From My Friends

Prod: M. Forest & G. Flynn

The basics of creating schools where all kids belong and learn together. Hands on strategies – MAPS & Circles of Friends.

Path: 2nd Edition

Planning Possible Positive Futures

Pearpoint, O'Brien, Forest

A guide to exciting, creative, colorful futures planning for families, organizations and schools to build caring "including" places to live, work & learn. Graphics unleash capacity. Path - an eight step problem solving approach involving dreaming and thinking backwards. Color graphic included!

TheAll Star Company

Building Teams — **People, Performance, Profit** — Team Building

Nick Marsh

An exciting book about BUILDING TEAMS and CHANGE. The All Star metaphor is about building powerful teams in your organization. Five Facets: Destiny–Vision; Ringmastery–Leadership; Encore–Marketplace; All Star Cast–People; Making a Difference–Values!

Kids, Disabilities and Regular Classrooms

An Annotated Bibliography of Selected Children's Literature on Disability

NEW! *Gary Owen Bunch* NEW!

An exciting guide to positive stories about children. An excellent resource for every classroom, family and human service organization.

All My Life's a Circle

Using the Tools: Circles, MAPS & PATH

M. Falvey, M. Forest, J. Pearpoint & R. Rosenberg

Introduction to circles, MAPS & PATH - a great place to start!

Changes in Latitude/Attitude

Inst. on Disability, NH

The Role of the Inclusion Facilitator - beautifully presented – the experience and wisdom of inclusion facilitators in New Hampshire.

Action for Inclusion

4th printing

by *O'Brien and Forest* with Pearpoint, Snow & Hasbury

Over 15,000 copies distributed – "A down to earth blueprint of what 21st century education ought to be doing for all kids in regular classrooms. Modest but powerful strategies for making it happen in a jargon -free, step-by-step book." Herb Lovett, Boston

L'Intégration en Action: Maintenant disponible en Français

From Behind the Piano

3rd printing

Building Judith Snow's Unique Circle of Friends

by *Jack Pearpoint* *afterword: John O'Brien*

This is the story of Judith Snow & her Joshua committee. It demonstrates that love, determination and hard work will conquer challenges. An inspiration for anyone struggling to make a difference.

Inclusion News

The Center's independent annual newspaper - articles & resources you need to keep you fully included. Get it! It has raving fans!

INCLUSION PRESS

ORDER FORM

24 Thome Crescent
Toronto, ON
Canada M6H 2S5
Tel 416-658-5363 Fax 416-658-5067
e-mail: 74640.1124@compuserve.com
WEB PAGE: http://inclusion.com

Together We're Better *Video*
Producer: Comforty Media Concepts
Staff Development Kit: a 2 hour video 3-pack of resources with Marsha Forest, Jack Pearpoint and Judith Snow demonstrating MAPS, PATH and CIRCLES. An inspiration.

Miller's MAP *Video*
Prod: Expectations Unltd &Inclusion Press
Children, parents, neighbors and professionals make inclusion happen– team facilitation and graphics in a MAP.

Friends of ...Clubs *Video*
Producers: Oregon Dept. of Education & University of Oregon A beautiful 15 min. story about creating community partnerships. Friends, friends, friends - the spark of life.

Dream Catchers *Video*
Producer: Institute on Disability, NH
New 16 minute video about dreams and circles of friends. Beautiful images, personal stories, images of the future. An inspiration.

Inclusion Exclusion Poster
by Jack Pearpoint A vibrant eye catching 18" X 24" graphic poster exploring the why behind Inclusion and Exclusion.

Lessons for Inclusion
Curriculum to Build Caring Elementary Classrooms - Inst. on Disability, U of MN
Step by step - day to day in elementary classrooms. Outstanding collection of curriculum ideas proven in classrooms in Minnesota.

Treasures **Inst. on Disability, NH**
Photo essay on friendship - images of children of New Hampshire explains how to include everyone. Just do it.

Reflections on Inclusive Education
Patrick Mackan C.R. Stories and reflections - for your family, assemblies, classrooms, church.

Don't Pass Me By: *Gary Bunch*
Writings from "street kids" labelled illiterate: "bad, sad, mad and can't add".

The Whole Community Catalogue
editor: D. Wetherow
Indispensable guide for building communities and supporting inclusion. Beautifully organized, chock full of ideas, quotes, resources.

Books		Copies	Total
Path Workbook - 2nd Edition Planning Positive Possible Futures	$12 + $3/copy shipping	___	___
Members of Each Other Building Community Together	$12 + $3/ copy shipping	___	___
The All Star Company It's About Building Teams!	$25 + $3/ copy shipping	___	___
Lessons for Inclusion Curriculum Ideas for Inclusion in Elementary Schools	$12 + $3/ copy shipping	___	___
Kids, Disabilities & Regular Classrooms Annotated Bibliography of Children's Literature on Disability	$12 + $3/ copy shipping	___	___
What's Really Worth Doing Judith Snow's new Book on Circles	$12 + $3/copy shipping	___	___
The Inclusion Papers - Strategies & Stories	$12 + $3/copy shipping	___	___
Changes in Latitudes/Attitudes Role of the Inclusion Facilitator	$12 + $3/ copy shipping	___	___
Treasures	$12 + $3/ copy shipping	___	___
All My Life's a Circle Booklet putting Circles, MAPS & PATH in Action	$12 + $3/ copy shipping	___	___
Reflections on Inclusive Education	$12 + $3/copy shipping	___	___
Don't Pass Me By	$12 + $3/copy shipping	___	___
Action for Inclusion The Classic on Inclusion	$12 + $3/copy shipping	___	___
Parcours: Path en francais	$12 + $3/copy shipping	___	___
L'Intégration en Action (en Français)	$12 + $3/copy shipping	___	___
From Behind the Piano Building Circles of Friends	$12 + $3/copy shipping	___	___
The Whole Community Catalogue Great Resource Catalogue - Indispensable	$12 + $3/copy shipping	___	___
Inclusion – Exclusion Poster (18 X 24)	$10 + $2/copy shipping	___	___
Inclusion News (free with book order)	$2 + $2 for shipping	___	___
Inclusion News in Bulk (box of 200)	$50 – includes shipping in NA	___	___
Videos			
*** NEW MAPS TRAINING VIDEO** Shafik's Map - step by step	$55 + $5 shipping	___	___
*** NEW FRIENDSHIP VIDEO** Judith, Marsha & Jack on friendship	$55 + $5 shipping	___	___
*** PATH TRAINING VIDEO** Path: Introductory Training Video	$55 + $5 shipping	___	___
PATH Demonstration Video (# 2) Follows PATH Training Video	$55 + $5 shipping	___	___
Dream Catchers (Dreams & Circles)	$55 + $5 shipping	___	___
Friends of ... Clubs -Friends, friends, friends	$55 + $5 shipping	___	___
Interdependence Teenagers Exploring Interdependence	$55 + $5 shipping	___	___
Miller's MAP - MAPS in Action	$55 + $5 shipping	___	___
With a Little Help from My Friends The Classic on Circles & MAPS	$55 + $5 shipping	___	___
Kids Belong Together MAPS & Circles	$55 + $5 shipping	___	___
Together We're Better (3 videos) Staff Development Kit	$175 + $10 shipping	___	___
	GRAND TOTAL		$=========

Bulk Orders: Phone! Shipping & Handling (over 10 items) 15%

Note: Shipping costs are for North America.

Prepayment on orders under $25 required. Prepayment speeds orders.

Name: ____________________
Organization: ____________________
Address: ____________________
City: ____________________
Prov./State ____________ Post Code/ZIP ________
Work Phone ____________ Cheque Enclosed ________
Home Phone ____________ Fax ________